THE LAW OF YOUR LAND

A Practical Guide To The New
CANADIAN CONSTITUTION

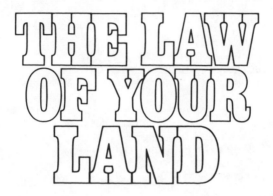

THE LAW
OF YOUR
LAND

J. Stuart Langford

Canadian Broadcasting Corporation

The Canada Act 1982 and The Constitution Act, 1982 reproduced by permission of the Minister of Supply and Services Canada.

Canadian Cataloguing in Publication Data
    Langford, J. Stuart (James Stuart), 1946–
        The law of your land

    Includes index.
    ISBN 0-88794-107-9

    1. Canada. 2. Canada—Constitutional law—
    Amendments. 3. Canada—Constitutional history.
    I. Title.
    KE4219.L36   342.71'035   C82-094545-5

Published by CBC Enterprises
Box 500, Station A
Toronto, Ontario
M5W 1E6

Managing Editor: Paula S. Goepfert
Copy Editor: Greg Ioannou
Designer: Keith Abraham
Cover Design: Garfield Reeves-Stevens
Indexer: Sara Jane Kennerley

Printed in Canada
1   2   3   4   5   86   85   84   83   82

To my wife, Jeanne

ACKNOWLEDGMENTS

A number of people helped make this book a reality. My wife, Jeanne, encouraged me to take on the project at a time when, after four years of covering the Constitution for CBC's The National, I was not sure that I could look at the subject one more time. Once committed to the writing I was pushed and pulled along the route to completion by two tireless supporters: Paula Goepfert, my editor, who helped make the book readable and Carolyn Brunton at CBC Enterprises who worked hard getting the book into print so people could read it. Along the way three Langfords, Warren, the civil servant, John, the professor, and Lynn, the lawyer, read various manuscript drafts and from their particular vantage points hunted down and helped eradicate errors.

Three others deserve special thanks. Trina McQueen, who in 1978 hired me to be CBC's legal correspondent and gave me the unique opportunity to cover the constitutional story; Elly Alboim, my assignment editor, who for four years made sure I got the story right; and Cameron Graham, my present boss, who has so patiently allowed the writing of this book to encroach on other duties.

Finally, a special albeit belated thanks to Barry Strayer who taught me constitutional law so many years ago and first got the blood running.

Contents

Introduction

Even before he became prime minister, Pierre Elliott Trudeau, first as law professor and then as member of Parliament and minister of justice, had been calling for constitutional reform. So long had he been trying to convince provincial premiers that constitutional changes were needed that in October 1980, after yet another first ministers conference had ended in failure, hardly anyone was surprised when Trudeau announced to the country that the federal government would do the job alone. With or without provincial consent, Ottawa would ask Britain to alter the Constitution, add an amending formula and a charter of rights and send the British North America Act home to Canada.

Trudeau's opponents in Parliament and in the provincial legislatures reacted with indignation. They accused the prime minister of violating the very tenets of Canadian federalism by proposing arbitrarily to change the structure of government. When Trudeau refused to return to the negotiating table eight of the premiers took their case to court. They started court of appeal actions in Manitoba, Newfoundland and Quebec. All posed the same basic question: Constitutionally, can the federal government ask Britain to amend and send home the BNA Act without provincial consent? The provinces lost in Manitoba, won in Newfoundland and then lost again in Quebec's appeal court. By the time the case went to the Supreme Court, many provincial representatives were privately convinced they'd lose there too. They won.

On 28 September 1981, the Supreme Court declared Trudeau's plans unconstitutional. In a six–three decision the Court admitted that there was nothing in the written part of the Constitution that prohibited the federal government from acting without provincial consent. But, the Court ruled, a good deal of Canada's Constitution does not exist in written form. Much of it exists only in the form of traditions or conventions, some of which have developed since Confederation. One such convention clearly prohibits unilateral federal action on matters of vital importance to the provinces. The Court's ruling led to further federal-provincial negotiations and, ultimately, to Canada's new Constitution.

If the September 28th judgment surprised the eight dissenting premiers and disappointed the prime minister, it confused much of the nation. How could the prime minister, two courts of appeal and the dozens of lawyers and constitutional experts that lined up on the federal side not have known that the Constitution forbade unilateral federal action? If the Supreme Court's judgment did nothing else, it reaffirmed that Canada's Constitution, the basic law of the land, is undefined and intangible. It is a steadily evolving body of rules, some written, some not, by which the country's system of democratic government functions.

Now that the Constitution is in Canada, the situation is no less confusing to the layman. Yesterday's Constitution dealt mainly with governments and institutions and with the relationships among them. Only in a very few instances (for example, in the areas of limited language rights) did it touch directly on people's lives. Today's Constitution will change all of that. It contains explicit guarantees of basic human rights and fundamental freedoms. But although it lists those guarantees, it does not spell out precisely what they mean.

Like the old Constitution, the new one will remain vague in many areas until time and circumstance permit its interpretation by the courts. That process, though, will likely take years. This book attempts to anticipate, to provide answers to some of the questions with which the new Constitution confronts Canadians. It is not a book for constitutional lawyers. It's not meant to tell you why the Constitution is as it is or why nearly 115 years of judicial review have produced one result and not another.

It addresses itself primarily to the question of how Canada's new Constitution differs from the old and how the changes in the fundamental law of the land will alter all our lives. Certainly our lives will be altered. It is quite impossible to bestow rights on people without some costs. For every right there is a corresponding duty. The rights newly acquired by women, the handicapped, the young and the old will force new responsibilities on all Canadians.

If women are at last to be recognized as truly equal, then hiring practices will have to change, sexual stereotyping will have to cease, labour laws, taxation laws and a host of others will have to be amended. If the handicapped demand the equality the Constitution promises them, then society will have to spend enormous sums of money to erase the obstacles, man-made and other, with which the handicapped are confronted daily.

The job of assessing exactly what the new Constitution means to us will fall squarely in the laps of Canada's judges. They will be faced with having to decide what exactly is meant by such notions as "the right to life" or "cruel and unusual punishment." If Canadians do not like what the courts decide, then the whole process of rewriting the Constitution will have to begin again and continue until finally the words in the document have been sufficiently reworked to describe the kind of society and nation Canadians want for themselves.

While the burden of interpreting the new Constitution will be borne by Canada's judges, parliamentarians and legislators will not be relieved of the problem of constitutional negotiations for some years to come. The Constitution is still in a quite embryonic form; it remains a political issue. To reach the compromise that is the new Constitution, Prime Minister Trudeau and the premiers made a commitment. They must meet again within a year to attempt to hammer out agreements on many of the issues that were too controversial to be settled in the hostile atmosphere of 1981. Native rights, the economy, communications, offshore resources, fisheries, family law and the reform of federal institutions such as the Senate and the Supreme Court are all on the agenda for the next constitutional conference of first ministers.

The next chapter in Canada's constitutional history will be an exciting one. It will bring to light some of the mysteries hidden in the new Charter of Rights and Freedoms; it may include a revamped division of powers, remodeled institutions and, conceivably, the working out of a completely new democratic process. Sovereign in both fact and theory, Canada is faced at last with the challenge of refining and testing the nationhood it has worked so long to achieve.

Yesterday's Constitution

In legal or political terms, the word *constitution* refers to a document that outlines the basic elements of a country's government. Typically, such a document contains a statement of the principles fundamental to that country's government, a description of the institutions designed to fulfill those principles and a list of the basic rights and freedoms guaranteed to every citizen. Between 1867 and 1982 no such document existed in Canada. For almost 115 years the Canadian Constitution consisted not of one all-encompassing statement but of a collection of laws, some written by politicians, some developed by judges and others that were to be found nowhere in written form but were the products of tradition and convention.

Some of the laws that made up the old Constitution were more easily identifiable than others. Those written by politicians were printed in the statute books of England and Canada. Those developed by judges took the form of court rulings, and the most important of these were recorded by official stenographers and then published in court reports. The unwritten parts of the old Constitution were honoured by observance, not publication. Such rules as those that govern the relationship between the prime minister and the cabinet or between the cabinet and the House of Commons fell into this latter category. The written parts of the old Constitution were perhaps the best known, but they were no more crucial to an understanding of the Canadian system of government than those rules spawned of custom and tradition.

THE WRITTEN LAWS

Because of Canada's historical ties to Great Britain, many of the statutes making up the written part of the old Constitution were British. Best known of these are the British North America Act of 1867, the subsequent amendments to that Act and the Statute of Westminster of 1931. But the written part of the old Constitution was not totally British. Canada's Parliament also contributed. The Saskatchewan Act and the Alberta Act, both passed in 1905, are just two of the Canadian laws that became part of the old Constitution. As well, it included a number of provincial statutes, such as the various provincial electoral acts. Finally, parts of the old Constitution were to be found in a number of Orders in Council, such as the 1873 Imperial Order in Council, which formally made Prince Edward Island a province of Canada.

Those written parts of the old Constitution that were composed by judges rather than politicians were less well known. These were the rules of common law. They were developed over centuries, first in British courts,* then Canadian, as judges, confronted with jurisdictional battles, struggled to delineate the apportionment of power among the crown, the executive and the legislative branches of government. The crown in Canada (for all practical purposes the governor general acting with the advice of the cabinet) derives much of its power from judge-made law. Some examples are the powers to grant clemency, to issue passports, to appoint ambassadors and even to declare war.

Of all this constitutional writing, political and judicial, one British law, the British North America Act of 1867, was indisputably the most important. So fundamental was it to the Canadian system of federalism that for nearly 115 years the BNA Act alone was popularly referred to as The Constitution. The BNA Act did four things:

1. It created Canada as a separate and nearly sovereign nation with, as the Act's preamble says, "a Constitution similar in Principle to that of the United Kingdom."
2. It set out the type of government by which Canada would be ruled by establishing the House of Commons, the Senate, the provincial legislatures and the offices of the governor general and the lieutenant governors as well as the basis of a judicial

---

*Until 1949 the court of last resort for Canadians was the judicial committee of the Privy Council in Britain. For this reason, it is necessary to examine the judicial decisions of both Canada and Britain in order to find all of the "judge-made" parts of the written Constitution.

system and the general rules governing election or appointment to those institutions.

3. It divided lawmaking power in Canada between Ottawa and the provinces.
4. Finally, it set out rules in a number of other areas, such as use of the French and English languages, control of education, ownership of natural resources, establishment of prisons and the admission of new provinces and territories to the Dominion of Canada.

Although many important laws, politically and judicially made, combined to make up the old Constitution, one other was so key to the foundation of Canada's sovereignty that it needs special mention. The Statute of Westminster (1931) was intended to complete what the BNA Act began by bestowing on Canada final legislative independence. With one exception, it did so. Only the power to amend Canada's Constitution remained in Britain after the passage of the Statute of Westminster.

The amending power was not withheld from Canada by a British government bent on retaining one last vestige of colonial sovereignty. In fact, the power to amend the Constitution was a colonial link that Britain specifically asked Canada to sever. Westminster wanted to make Canada's independence complete by the 1931 statute, but some provincial leaders objected. At a 1927 constitutional conference the prime minister and the premiers had been unable to work out a Canadian amending formula agreeable to all of them. Some premiers feared that Ottawa would manipulate an all-Canadian amending formula and use it to encroach upon the jurisdiction of the provinces. To guard against that eventuality the premiers asked Britain to retain the amending power.

One common thread ran through the many written parts of the old Constitution: Of all the hundreds of clauses of British and Canadian statutes and of all the hundreds of pages of judicial pronouncements, only a handful dealt directly with the people of Canada. Nearly all of the written parts of the old Constitution dealt with governments. Institutions were created and defined, principles governing those institutions were enunciated and power was distributed among institutions and between levels of government. Almost nowhere in the old Constitution were the rights and freedoms of citizens delineated. The sorts of personal guarantees and protections that are so fundamental to the Constitution of the United States of America, for example, were conspicuous in the written part of Canada's old Constitution only by their absence.

THE UNWRITTEN CONSTITUTION

Nevertheless, inalienable civil rights did exist in Canada under the old Constitution. They formed part of that "other" Canadian Constitution, the unwritten rules of democracy that have their roots in British customs and conventions dating back to the Magna Charta. Canadians have long taken for granted the fundamental elements of democracy and basic human rights that were not contained anywhere in the written portion of the old Constitution. Their faith was not unjustified. Canadian history contains many examples of the courts recognizing these principles as fundamental to the law of the land and repelling legislative attacks against them.

In 1937 the Social Credit government of William ("Bible Bill") Aberhart became concerned about what Aberhart construed as biased reporting in Alberta. The premier believed that the province's newspapers were unfairly reflecting the purpose and effect of his government's policies and legislation. To rectify this situation the Alberta government introduced a law entitled An Act To Ensure Publication Of Accurate News And Information. It was a barely disguised attempt to censor the province's newspapers.

The Press Bill, as it became known, gave the Alberta government unheard of powers over news and editorial writing in the province. Newspapers were required to publish government-supplied statements describing government activities and policies. As well, upon request newspapers were obliged to furnish the government with the names and addresses of the writers and sources of any editorial, article or news item contained in any issue of the paper. The government was empowered to order any newspaper closed or publication of any portion of a newspaper suspended. All violations were punishable as criminal offences.

The Supreme Court struck down the Press Bill saying it violated an unwritten part of the Constitution, the right to freedom of discussion. That right, the Court declared, was so fundamental to the concept of democracy in Canada that its existence predated even the BNA Act. The *Press Bill* decision reads in part:

> Under the British system, which is ours, no political party can erect a probitionary barrier to prevent the electors from getting information concerning the policy of the government. Freedom of discussion is essential to enlightened public opinion in a democratic State; it cannot be curtailed without affecting the right of the people to be informed through sources independent

of the government concerning matters of public interest. There must be an untrammelled publication of the news and political opinions of the political parties contending for ascendancy.

The thirties produced another law that threatened the free flow of information and, in the opinion of those opposed to it, freedom of religion. This was a Quebec City bylaw enacted in 1933, which stated in part:

It is, by the present by-law forbidden to distribute in the streets of the City of Quebec, any book, pamphlet, booklet, circular, tract whatever without having previously obtained for so doing the written permission of the Chief of Police.

The Jehovah's Witnesses in Quebec challenged the law as an attempt to deprive them of their right to preach the Christian gospel both by word of mouth and by distribution of printed matter. One of the sect's members, a Mr. Saumur, was arrested and imprisoned under the law for distributing religious literature. When the matter finally came before the Supreme Court of Canada in 1953, counsel for the City of Quebec admitted that the bylaw was directed against the contents of the printed materials handed out on Quebec streets by the Jehovah's Witnesses.

In declaring the Quebec bylaw to be invalid, the Court quoted with approval the earlier ruling in the Alberta *Press Bill* case and then declared that the same unwritten Constitution that guaranteed freedom of discussion also protected freedom of religion. In the words of Mr. Justice Locke:

The appellant in the present matter has exercised what, in my opinion, is his constitutional right to the practice of his religious profession and mode of worship . . .

Rulings such as those in the *Saumur* and *Press Bill* cases were sources both of encouragement and of frustration for Canadian civil rights advocates. Their spirits were naturally enough buoyed by the judicial identification and substantiation of freedom of discussion and religion as basic rights but, at the same time, a gnawing doubt about how many other such fundamental rights existed made it difficult to celebrate the Court rulings as total victories over oppression. There were other cases and other successes for Canada's civil rights champions, but each case was decided on its own merits. Each case identified a fundamental right or freedom and each case corroborated the fact that, indeed, an unwritten list of constitutionally protected rights existed. But that was all.

What the Supreme Court never did was list all of the rights and freedoms that existed in the unwritten part of the old Constitution. The Court felt bound by what is called "the principle of judicial economy," which essentially restricts a judge to a discussion of only the minimum amount of law necessary to decide the case before him. Because of this principle, Canadians were left with only a limited knowledge of their civil rights and how well these were safeguarded. They knew an unwritten code of rights and freedoms existed, and they knew the courts would protect those rights and freedoms if they were threatened. Still, they never learned what all the rights and freedoms were.

Over the years it also became clear that the unwritten parts of the old Constitution dealt with more than just people's rights and freedoms. The Court looked to convention and tradition, as well, for many of the rules regulating institutional proceedings and intergovernmental relations. Some of the most fundamental rules of Canadian parliamentary democracy were nowhere to be found in the written part of the old Constitution. For example, it is only by convention that the government must resign if the opposition obtains a majority at the polls. That rule is not found in the BNA Act, the Statute of Westminster or any other constitutional document.

The most recent important judicial reference to the binding nature of unwritten constitutional conventions came in September 1981. The year before, in the fall of 1980, the federal government announced that it had given up trying to reach a federal-provincial consensus on constitutional reform. Yet another first ministers conference on the Constitution had failed to produce agreement, so Ottawa decided to move alone, to ask Britain to amend the BNA Act and send it to Canada without provincial consent. Alarmed by what they regarded as a violation of the basic principles of Canadian federalism, eight of the provinces challenged the federal government in court.

Nowhere in the old Constitution was there spelled out a proper procedure for formulating a request for change. Traditionally, such requests had taken the form of a joint resolution of the House of Commons and the Senate to the Queen and through her to Westminster. But, also by tradition, such resolutions had always been supported by the provinces if the changes requested in them affected provincial powers. The Supreme Court of Canada declared the federal government's plans unconstitutional saying that they violated the established convention that major amendments to the BNA Act must always be supported by substantial provincial consent. The Court summed up Canada's Constitution in the form of a mathematical equation: "Constitutional conventions plus constitutional law equal the total constitution of the country."

That equation may accurately define the old Constitution, but it did little to make it more palatable to those politicians who sought to change it. For them the old Constitution was both a legal and political hodgepodge. The written sections were partially British, partially Canadian, partially drafted by politicians, partially by judges. The unwritten parts were legally binding but still, after 114 years of Confederation, intangible and ambiguous. Even after dozens of court challenges the scope and power of the unwritten part of the old Constitution had not been plumbed. The situation was simply too uncertain, and for many politicians nothing could be a more unseemly constitutional characteristic than uncertainty.

THE 114-YEAR WAR

Uncertainty alone, however, was not sufficient to force rapid constitutional reform, at least not rapid reform on a major scale. To be sure, the Constitution was amended between 1867 and 1982 but only to accomplish limited goals, for example, to admit Newfoundland as a new province (1949), to give the western provinces control over natural resources (1930), to transfer to the federal government exclusive control over unemployment insurance (1940), to alter the tenure of superior court judges (1960). What eluded Canadian politicians was a general agreement to end the uncertainty by writing a new constitution, a clear, concise and complete constitution that would leave nothing to chance, nothing to the whim of future lawmakers or law enforcers.

The vagueness of the old Constitution was more than a source of frustration. It also made the bargaining process needed to hammer out a new one very difficult. Bargaining perhaps sounds like an unusual way to describe intergovernmental negotiations, but a good deal of federal-provincial constitutional negotiation comes down to exactly that. Because much of the old Constitution was devoted to dividing power between federal and provincial lawmakers, much of the discussion leading to a new Constitution was about a new division of power. In colloquial terms, "Who gets what?" was the major topic at any federal-provincial constitutional conference.

But so unclear was the old Constitution that discussion of "Who gets what" often got not farther than trying to agree on who had what. These problems were not caused solely by the unwritten parts of the old Constitution. The major element of the written part, the BNA Act, also presented difficulties. Written in 1867, the BNA Act predated inventions such as radio, television, satellite communication and computers.

As new inventions opened up new areas of jurisdiction, both federal and provincial politicians claimed power over them. Almost invariably, the courts were called upon to decide which claim was the strongest. Sometimes Ottawa won, sometimes the provinces. The uncertainty bothered both sides, but it also made both sides reluctant to bargain away even the smallest power base. The lessons of history were too vivid to ignore. For example, in 1867 communications was a miniscule area of jurisdiction under federal control. It amounted to no more than a very limited telegraph capability. If, in the effort to negotiate a new division of power, Ottawa had traded communications to the provinces in the early part of this century, it would have given up control of what in the past quarter century has become one of the fastest growing fields of legislative jurisdiction.

Disagreement on the issue of control was not limited to ''Who gets what.'' As well, there has always been in Canada a philosophical controversy over who should logically and properly have control over *most of the lawmaking power.* This issue of control, both specific and philosophical, seemed to frustrate every attempt to achieve major constitutional reform.

At the root of the problem were two diametrically opposed views of what Canadian federalism really means. Is Canada a centralist state where most decision making emanates from Ottawa, as federal representatives argue, or is it decentralized, a country composed of many strong regional voices, as the provinces contend? As long as this issue remains unresolved, and it is far from settled today, renegotiating the division of power between Ottawa and the provinces will be a difficult process, indeed.

A strong argument can be made for the view that when the Fathers of Confederation created the Dominion of Canada in 1867, they modelled it on the highly centralized British system where Parliament is supreme. According to this theory, provincial governments were established in the first place only as a convenience to the federal government. The size of the country made it impractical not to establish some sort of local councils so that the federal government could be free from the burden of strictly regional concerns. Provincial governments, so the theory goes, were not intended to wield real power but only to deal with local problems. The very preamble to the BNA Act gives some credence to the supremacy of Parliament theory:

WHEREAS the Provinces of Canada, Nova Scotia and New Brunswick have expressed their Desire to be federally united into one Dominion under the Crown of the United Kingdom of Great Britain and Ireland, with a Constitution similar in Principle to that of the United Kingdom . . .

Decentralists in Canada acknowledge that the original intent of the Fathers of Confederation may well have been to reflect in Canadian federalism the image of the British parliamentary system. However, they argue, that intent, if it ever existed, was never translated into practice. In reality, provincial governments were never relegated to second-class status. From the very beginning, Canada has had its own brand of evenly balanced federalism—a collection of governments each paramount in certain areas of lawmaking but none inferior to the others.

Given the enormous philosophical gulf that has existed for so long between Ottawa and the provinces, it is little wonder that they have found it difficult to forge an agreement on major constitutional reform. Talks have always broken down over the same issues: visions of Canada and the redivision of power. Federal government representatives want most of the power to emanate from Ottawa. This, they argue, would ensure stability. If Ottawa made all the laws, every Canadian would be subject to the same rules and regulations. Country-wide uniformity would mean that no Canadian would feel disadvantaged because of residence.

From the provincial point of view, strict centralism in a country as diverse as Canada is a formula for disaster. More power in Ottawa, they argue, means less sensitivity to regional differences, to the wide range of viewpoints that make up the Canadian mosaic. Decentralists feel that most of the power should reside with provincial governments. That, they say, is the level of government most in tune with local mores and needs and, therefore, best able to pass sound, responsive legislation.

What, then, enabled Ottawa and the provinces to finally reach an agreement on a new Constitution in November 1981? Certainly, it was not a conversion of one side to the other's philosophical position. Before and after the agreement the federal government remained committed to the centralist viewpoint. Most provinces remained adamant that decentralization was crucial. What happened in November was that the redivision of power was dropped as an issue. Spurred on by public annoyance with constitutional squabbling and by a clear directive from the Supreme Court that the new Constitution had to grow out of a substantial federal-provincial agreement, the two levels of government set aside the contentious question of who gets what and concentrated on finding a limited consensus on patriation, an amending formula and a charter of rights.

Patriation was easy. Everyone wanted the Constitution home. The problems rose only when the first ministers began to discuss how the Constitution should be changed before it was domiciled in Canada. Chief among provincial conditions for patriation was that the Constitution come home with an amending formula that did not give Ottawa excessive power to make future changes.

Finding an amending formula was not easy. The premiers insisted on a clause allowing them to opt out of certain future amendments if they felt such amendments would be of little or no benefit to them. For example, under the opt-out provision an amendment that transferred power over education to Ottawa could be avoided by as many as three provinces. They could opt out of the amendment and retain power over education while the other seven provinces agreed and handed jurisdiction over to Ottawa.

The federal government disliked the opting-out provision proposal intensely because, it said, the scheme would ultimately result in a country with ten different constitutions. Every time a province opted out, that province's constitution would become slightly different from that of its neighbours. After fifty or a hundred years the slight variances could add up to a completely different constitution in each province. Without putting aside these reservations, Ottawa ultimately agreed to the provincial opt-out amending formula. Ottawa's agreement was one half of a trade-off. The provinces got the formula they preferred and the federal government got its much sought after Charter of Rights and Freedoms.

It was not that provincial leaders did not want civil rights protected. They did and they do. The issue in the minds of those opposed to the Charter was not "if" rights and freedoms should be protected but "how." Some premiers were vehemently opposed to enshrining human rights in the Constitution because, they argued, once placed there they could not easily be changed. Rights and freedoms, said some premiers, were best protected by provincial human rights codes, codes that can easily be amended as values change in the community. Clauses in a constitution are nearly cast in cement. If the courts interpret them in ways the politicians never intended, only the complicated and uncertain process of constitutional negotiation can correct the problem. One final compromise brought agreement: The federal government agreed to include a clause in the Charter enabling the provincial governments to vary the effect of certain parts of the Charter in their own provinces. All the premiers (all, that is, but Quebec's René Lévesque) agreed to adopt the Charter.

So, after 114 years the old Constitution was finally to be replaced, or more accurately, amended, enlarged and brought home to Canada. Agreement was possible only because Ottawa and the provinces put off the problem of dividing power until another day. The centralists and decentralists were able to find substantial agreement as the Supreme Court had required, but they were brought no closer together philosophically.

Today's Constitution

The Constitution that the first ministers agreed to in November 1981 contains the same basic elements as the one Prime Minister Trudeau had threatened to force on the dissident premiers the year before. It retains the unwritten parts of the old Constitution and it restructures the written part to include

- Most of the written parts of the old Constitution
- A strengthening of provincial control over natural resources
- A Charter of Rights and Freedoms, including language rights
- The recognition of native rights
- A commitment to the principle of equalization or revenue sharing between rich and poor provinces
- Provision for a future constitutional conference
- An amending formula
- A "schedule" or list containing the names of all past constitutional laws and showing whether those laws are now repealed, amended or unchanged.

Although the basic elements are those Prime Minister Trudeau wanted, the exact nature of each element is in many instances considerably altered. The hallmarks of federal-provincial compromise are everywhere to be seen in the new Constitution. The effects of that compromise are most noticeable in the following areas:

- Large portions of the Charter of Rights and Freedoms can be avoided by simple legislation.
- Special concessions are provided for Quebec in the minority language educational rights provisions.
- Native rights are not as clearly protected as they were in the earlier version.
- Revenue sharing guidelines are vaguer than they were in the earlier version.
- The amending formula contains a clause allowing provincial governments to opt out of certain future amendments.

Even with all the changes, the new Constitution can be regarded as a genuine breakthrough in the field of federal-provincial relations. After 115 years the country has become a truly sovereign nation with a Constitution domiciled and amendable in Canada and with a Charter of Rights and Freedoms that, despite opting out provisions, offers a laudable number of basic civil guarantees. All power now resides with either the federal or provincial governments. The last legal fetter tying Canada to England is cut while at the same time traditional Canadian fidelity to the British monarch remains intact.

THE BRITISH TIE

The history of the rapid rise and slow decline of the British Empire documents almost every conceivable route between colonialism and nationhood. Our neighbour to the south, for example, cut its colonial tie in 1776 by violent revolution. More recently Rhodesia, under the leadership of Ian Smith, fell out with Britain over the issue of racial equality and attempted to attain nationhood by unilaterally declaring independence. The Canadian experience was far less dramatic. Our Fathers of Confederation indicated a desire to sever the colonial link, the proper papers (the BNA Act) were drawn up, and Canada became a separate country.

Unfortunately, the guidelines set out for Canada in the BNA Act were soon out of date. The country expanded; new technologies developed; Canada went to war and afterwards took part in reshaping the world order. As 1867 retreated farther into history it became more and more apparent that Canada was nothing like the country that had been given limited sovereignty by the Parliament at Westminster through the BNA Act. As times changed, Canadians sought amendments to the Act but, because it was a British law, those amendments had to be sanctioned by Westminster. For over one hundred years

Canada had to formally request Westminster to make each desired change. The procedure, while largely ceremonial, did not sit well with Canadian nationalists. The new Constitution ends that last remaining requirement of colonial subservience forever.

Constitutional authorities correctly point out, however, that in strict legal theory the notion of forever cutting the British tie is a fiction. The problem is that in order to get the Constitution home Canada had to ask Britain one last time to pass the appropriate legislation amending the BNA Act.* Like all British laws defining Anglo-Canadian relations, this last one could theoretically be changed later by another less sympathetic Parliament at Westminster. Therefore, reason the experts, short of unilaterally declaring independence Canada can never be free of its bonds to the mother country. The argument, while legally correct, ignores the realities of international law and politics.

THE BRITISH NORTH AMERICA ACT TODAY

Despite a face lift, a name change** and new citizenship, the British North America Act is very much alive and operative in Canada. Its role today is precisely what it was in 1867, though the new Constitution contains a number of clauses designed to repair some of the BNA Act's deficiencies. As it always has the BNA Act continues to establish Canada as a federal state, provide brief descriptions of its institutions and their roles, set out certain rules that delineate the rights of government and citizens and, most important of all, divide the power to make laws between the federal and provincial levels of government. This latter role is all important because it is the foundation of the legal ordering of government functions in Canada. However, because the division of power was made in 1867, it demonstrates little sensitivity to the developments of the twentieth century.

This shortcoming is most clearly demonstrated by the growth of provincial influence since 1867. Through federal-provincial agreement rather than by constitutional assignment the provinces have assumed enormous power over economic and social policy in Canada. They are

---

*Britain granted the request by passing the Canada Act 1982, a four-section statute that adopted all of the provisions of the Constitution Act 1982 and terminated forever Britain's power to legislate for Canada. The Canada Act 1982 is reprinted at the end of this book.
**On 17 April 1982 the British North America Act was officially renamed the *Constitution Act 1867*. For clarity, however, this book refers to the BNA Act by its old name throughout.

active in energy development, pricing and taxation, and in a host of other areas that are national in dimension. Yet section 92, which lists the areas of exclusive provincial power, gives them *no* influence over matters of national significance.

The subjects listed in section 92 are almost entirely local in nature. They accord provincial governments only very limited power in such crucial areas as taxation, trade and commerce, natural resources, communications and transportation. If the provinces were restricted to the power base assigned to them in the BNA Act their influence would be reduced in scope to that of a modern municipality.

In contrast, the Constitution supplies Ottawa with a number of wide-sweeping legislative tools that give the federal government the power to dominate national policy making. Section 91 of the BNA Act bestows on Parliament either the exclusive or the dominant power in a number of legislative areas. The following list is a sample:

— The regulation of trade and commerce
— The borrowing of money on public credit
— National defence
— Navigation and shipping
— Sea coast and inland fisheries
— Currency and coinage
— Banking
— Interest
— Natives and land claims
— Immigration
— Marriage and divorce
— Criminal law

In addition to the above list, which again is not exhaustive, the BNA Act provides Ottawa with another powerful legislative device. The opening lines of section 91 say that Parliament has the right to pass any laws it deems necessary "for the Peace, Order, and good Government of Canada." The only stated limit to the use of the Peace, Order, and good Government lawmaking power is that no legislation passed in accordance with it may encroach upon any of the fifteen areas of exclusive jurisdiction given to the provinces in section 92.

In reality, this limitation has been circumvented by careful legal draftsmanship. In the years since Confederation Ottawa has used the Peace, Order, and good Government power to pass laws in a number of areas that appear to be provincial in nature. In 1882 and again in 1946 the federal government passed prohibition legislation despite the fact that the BNA Act gives the provinces control over the sale of alcoholic beverages. Between 1867 and 1975, Ottawa has used the Peace, Order, and good Government power to justify many actions, ranging from federal control over radio and aeronautics to the implementation of wage and price controls.

Initially, it was believed that the Peace, Order, and good Government provision was intended to provide an emergency power for use only in circumstances so dire that they threatened the well-being of the nation. Gradually, however, the courts relaxed this interpretation. Now, Ottawa can justify almost any form of legislation so long as it is national in scope. Only the most flagrant attempt to encroach upon provincial jurisdiction over purely local matters cannot be justified under the Peace, Order, and good Government power.

Because the courts appear to be so willing to consider almost any federal law valid under Peace, Order, and good Government, the provinces want the power abolished. It is the symbol, according to provincial representatives, of all that is wrong with the BNA Act—an Act that they say is so anachronistic and vague that it makes sensible modern government almost impossible.

Certainly, the division of power in the BNA Act is far from clear. Nowhere is that failing more obvious than in the field of natural resource ownership, management and sales. The BNA Act gives provincial governments total control over resources, such as oil and gas, so long as they remain in the ground or are stored in the province. Once they are put into pipelines, trucks or tank cars to be sold outside the province, power shifts. The oil and gas are no longer regarded as natural resources but as commodities for sale. Under the BNA Act, the federal government has the power to regulate the flow, price and taxation of commodities sold outside a province's boundaries.

The Constitution Act 1982 attempts to clarify the BNA Act's rather confusing division of power in the field of natural resources, as well as to make that division more realistic. It amends the BNA Act by adding a new heading of provincial power, section 92A, which reaffirms provincial ownership of natural resources and gives provincial governments greater power over the production, export and taxation of them. Although this section is welcomed by the producing provinces, many feel it does not go nearly far enough. They are disappointed because the new section makes provincial export regulations legal only if they do not conflict with federal laws. As well, the new provincial taxation powers may not be used discriminately. That means that if a province places a tax on exported natural resources it must also tax locally consumed resources at the same rate. Still, section 92A is a breakthrough. Provinces are finally given a constitutionally guaranteed voice in national policy decisions. Such input will be restricted by ultimate federal authority, but it is a beginning.

THE CHARTER OF RIGHTS AND FREEDOMS

Added to the old Constitution, the major parts of which are still in force, is the so-called "people's package"—the Charter of Rights and Freedoms. The Charter consists of thirty-four brand new constitutional provisions that for the first time in Canadian history place in the written Constitution a list of fundamental rights and freedoms. The list contains a number of familiar human rights protections, such as the rights to life and liberty and the right to vote in elections, but it also goes beyond the familiar. For example, women are guaranteed complete equality in all aspects of Canadian life, full protection against discrimination is extended to handicapped persons and discrimination based on age is outlawed. Taken as a whole, the Charter represents so progressive an approach to the protection of civil liberties that it has been hailed by representatives of every political stripe in Canada as one of the best in the world.

The Charter enshrines seven categories of rights and freedoms in the new Constitution.

1. *Fundamental Freedoms.* These are the freedoms of conscience, religion, thought, belief, opinion, expression, association and peaceable assembly, as well as freedom of the press.
2. *Democratic Rights.* These are the right to vote and run for office and the guarantee of regular democratic elections.
3. *Mobility Rights.* These are the right to live and work in any part of Canada.
4. *Legal Rights.* These are the right to life, liberty and security of the person; the right to be secure against unreasonable search and seizure; the right not to be arbitrarily detained or imprisoned; the right on arrest to be told why, to retain counsel and to challenge detainment. As well, extensive rules for fair trials are listed.
5. *Equality Rights.* This section bans discrimination based on race, national or ethnic origin, colour, religion, sex, age or mental or physical disability.
6. *Language Rights.* English and French are designated the official languages in all federal institutions and in New Brunswick.

Bilingual provisions already applicable to Quebec and Manitoba continue in force.

7. *Minority Language Educational Rights.* This sets out a formula for determining who has the right to be educated in French or English based on a "where numbers warrant" test.

As well, the Charter contains other sections allowing Canadians to rely on any other right that exists in Canada, recognizing the multicultural nature of the country and retaining all existing constitutional guarantees for denominational, separate or dissentient schools in Canada.

What the practical impact of the Charter on the everyday lives of Canadians will be is impossible to predict. Without question, our lives will be changed, but the extent of that change may take years to determine. Two aspects of the Charter guarantee that a lengthy and complex process of interpretation and clarification is ahead of us before we can confidently say, "The Charter of Rights and Freedoms guarantees me *this right.*"

First, the language of the Charter is often unclear or vague. Most difficult to assess is the effect of the many qualifiers that appear throughout it. For example, the whole Charter is subject to "such reasonable limits prescribed by law as can be demonstrably justified in a free and democratic society." What that means is almost anyone's guess. A number of the legal rights in the Charter are intended to protect Canadians against arbitrary and unreasonable police activities. But what is arbitrary? What is unreasonable? Do the tests vary? Is it reasonable for a policeman to shoot at a fleeing murder suspect? A fleeing purse snatcher? A fleeing jaywalker? The list of unanswered questions is a long one.

Second, and perhaps most worrisome to the people who fought so hard to see human rights placed in the Constitution, is that both levels of government have the power to nullify some of the Charter's protections. Either Parliament or a provincial legislature can pass a law violating Fundamental Freedoms (section 2), Legal Rights (sections 7-14) or Equality Rights (section 15) so long as that law specifically states that it is to take effect "notwithstanding"—or in spite of—the protections in the Charter. This "notwithstanding" provision is found in section 33.

Section 33 was added to the Charter during the November 1981 constitutional conference at the insistence of a number of the premiers. They did not want to lose the power to pass discriminatory legislation in special circumstances. For example, Saskatchewan premier Allan

Blakeney regarded it as unthinkable that an elderly widow who needed to rent rooms in her home so as to make ends meet should have no power to refuse to rent to men. Other premiers felt that some of the Legal Rights in the Charter might make it next to impossible for police and crown attorneys to successfully investigate and prosecute suspected criminals.

Prime Minister Trudeau and those premiers opposed to section 33 contended that if constitutionally enshrined rights are to offer real protection for Canadians they must apply equally everywhere in the country. In the end a compromise was hammered out. Section 33 was included in the Charter but subsection (3) placed a limit of five years on any "notwithstanding" legislation. This "sunset clause" forces any government wishing to limit rights or freedoms to publicly debate such legislation in the House of Commons or a legislature every five years. The rationale is that few governments will risk trying to pass limitations if public opinion is against them.

It is important to emphasize that not all of the Charter is subject to "notwithstanding" legislation. Only three parts—Fundamental Freedoms, Legal Rights and Equality Rights—fall into the category of guarantees that can be avoided. The rest are binding on all levels of government and cannot be reduced by normal legislation.

Although no one can say precisely how the Charter will change our lives, many eminent groups and individuals have tried to predict the effects of specific sections. Much has been said in Parliament and in the special joint committee of the Senate and the House of Commons that studied the new constitutional provisions between November 1980 and February 1981. Too, the written presentations of interest groups that lobbied for the retention, removal or alteration of various clauses and of academics who studied the Charter provide insight. The explanations of individual sections that follow draw on this formidable collection of spoken and written commentary and offer, so far as is possible, a glimpse at the future.

The Preamble

Whereas Canada is founded upon principles that recognize the supremacy of God and the rule of law:

In terms of legislative impact, the preamble is of little effect. The numbered sections of the Charter of Rights and Freedoms are conclusive both in what they direct and what they forbid. Thus, the recognition of the supremacy of God, for example, does not detract from the right of an atheist to the "freedom of conscience and religion" guaranteed under section 2.

Only if a section of an act is ambiguous does a court look to the preamble for direction. Because freedom of religion has always been basic to Canadian democracy, there is little likelihood that the Christian complexion of the preamble will have the effect of limiting religious freedom for atheists or non-Christians.

The recognition in the preamble of the rule of law must be regarded in the same way as the recognition of the supremacy of God. Only if a section raises unanswerable doubts about the way Canadians should be treated in the courts or about whether or not the provisions in the Charter apply equally to all might this aspect of the preamble be referred to by a judge charged with clearing up those doubts. No section of the Charter appears to violate the concept of equal treatment that is fundamental to the rule of law and so it is unlikely that the mention of the principle in the preamble will have any effect.

Guarantee of Rights and Freedoms

> Section 1. The *Canadian Charter of Rights and Freedoms* guarantees the rights and freedoms set out in it subject only to such reasonable limits prescribed by law as can be demonstrably justified in a free and democratic society.

Section 1 is called a "guarantee." Its purpose, however, is not to strengthen the Charter's protections. Rather, it is intended to give both federal and provincial governments the power to limit rights and freedoms so long as no limitation offends the spirit of democracy. For example, freedom of expression and freedom of peaceful assembly are guaranteed in section 2, but laws banning defamation, hate messages, riots and even unruly behaviour on picket lines appear to fall within the definition of "reasonable limits" contained in section 1. The rationale underlying this first section is that no one may exercise his or her rights and freedoms in such a way as to violate the rights and freedoms of others. It seems clear that section 1 also anticipates situations where everyone's civil liberties can either be weakened or suspended completely. Just when such blanket suspensions would be "reasonable" is another question altogether.

Most commentators agree that section 1 would not prevent Parliament from invoking the War Measures Act in a situation that duplicated the unrest of the October Crisis of 1970. In the event of a national crisis the government could take steps to limit whatever rights or freedoms it considered necessary to prevent the destruction of democracy and civil order. In the event of something less than a national crisis, however, Parliament's power is less clear. Until the Supreme Court is faced with an instance of a government using section 1 to limit rights and freedoms, it is difficult to know what the justices will consider justifiable government intervention.

One point is clear: Section 1 requires Parliament or a legislature to justify any limitation of rights and freedoms. The underlying assumption is that the guarantees in the Charter are inviolate unless infringement upon them can be proved essential. For example, if the War Measures Act were employed, the burden of demonstrating why it should be allowed would be on Parliament. Those challenging the limitations would be taken to be correct until proved wrong.

Civil liberties advocates are watching this section closely. The forty-one groups and individuals that commented on the notion of a government being empowered to limit rights and freedoms were unanimous in their opinion that any limitation power should be employed only in dire circumstances. Although they seem content with the wording of the section, they remain cautious. The real problem with any limitation section is that by the time it becomes apparent that it is too broadly worded, it is too late. Only after people have lost their rights and freedoms are they certain that the laws protecting them were not strong enough.

Fundamental Freedoms

Section 2. Everyone has the following fundamental freedoms:
(a) freedom of conscience and religion;
(b) freedom of thought, belief, opinion and expression, including freedom of the press and other media of communication;
(c) freedom of peaceful assembly; and
(d) freedom of association.

At first glance this section appears to be a rather innocuous restatement of freedoms that the majority of Canadians would never question. In fact, the controversy generated by this list of freedoms has been substantial. Some interest groups want it narrowed, others, broadened. These examples demonstrate the problem: The Canadian Jewish Congress is concerned that freedom of speech may be interpreted by the courts so as to make hate propaganda legal. A similar concern has been voiced by the National Black Coalition of Canada and a number of other minority groups. The Mennonite Central Committee wanted the freedom of religion guarantee strengthened and clarified so that both individuals and *groups* would be guaranteed freedom from oppression. The committee fears that the present wording restricts the freedom to individuals. The Canadian Association of Chiefs of Police, on the other hand, thinks the wording is too broad. It wanted "freedom of conscience" limited so as to exclude protection for cults whose practices include morals crimes or the use of drugs.

These concerns and others caused some provincial premiers to demand the inclusion of section 2 in the list of rights and freedoms that can be avoided by the use of notwithstanding legislation passed under section 33. There is a belief among some politicians that the guarantees of freedom of peaceful assembly and of freedom of association may render illegal certain provincial and municipal laws governing demonstrations or picket line activities. Their concerns may be misplaced. It is possible that present labour laws and crowd-control bylaws are "justified" under the terms of section 1. However, if the courts rule that the freedoms in section 2 can be limited only in real emergencies some provinces will probably move quickly to pass their own notwithstanding exceptions to the rule.

Democratic Rights

Democratic rights are set out in sections 3, 4 and 5 of the Charter. Canadian citizens are guaranteed the rights to vote and to run for elected office, both federally and provincially. Except in times of national emergency, such as war, invasion or insurrection, no House of Commons and no legislative assembly may continue longer than five years. Finally, there must be a sitting of Parliament and each legislature at least once every year. So basic are these rights and obligations that it is highly unlikely that the courts will ever be asked to interpret them.

Mobility Rights

Mobility rights were hotly debated in the course of constitutional negotiations, and the section of the Constitution that now describes these rights, section 6, is the product of an intricate compromise.

The key provision under the Mobility Rights heading is contained in subsection (2), which reads

Section 6. (2) Every citizen of Canada and every person who has the status of a permanent resident of Canada has the right

> (a) to move to and take up residence in any province; and
> (b) to pursue the gaining of a livelihood in any province.

The objective of this subsection is to remedy, at least partially, the growing trend toward economic isolationism among the provinces. Newfoundland's ban against out-of-province oilrig workers and Quebec's discrimination against non-Quebec construction workers are causing considerable concern among those politicians who want the country to operate as a single economic unit. They fear that Canada's greatest assets—size, natural resources and diversity—will be weakened by artificial trade barriers.

Those who oppose any form of provincial self-favouritism wanted a third guarantee added to the guarantees of the right to live and work anywhere in the country: They wanted all Canadians to have the right to own property anywhere in Canada. This was blocked by the efforts of representatives from Prince Edward Island, which restricts the amount of waterfront property non-Islanders can own, and by representatives of Saskatchewan, which is worried about non-Saskatchewan interests buying up large tracts of farmland.

Provincial pressure brought about two additions to the Mobility Rights section. First, subsection (3) was added. It reads

> Section 6. (3) The rights specified in subsection (2) are subject to
> (a) any laws or practices of general application in force in a province other than those that discriminate among persons primarily on the basis of province of present or previous residence; and
> (b) any laws providing for reasonable residency requirements as a qualification for the receipt of publicly provided social services.

This two-part clause upholds the right of provincial governments to pass laws governing trades and professions and to restrict free access to them so long as the restrictions are applicable to everyone, not just nonresidents. Thus, entrance requirements for lawyers, doctors, plumbers and auto mechanics will not be negated by subsection (2), which gives all Canadians the right to work and live in any province. As well, subsection (3) allows provinces to set residency requirements as qualifications for receiving social services. This gives provincial governments a method of stopping a large inflow of nonresidents who might be induced by higher welfare payments or other social services to relocate.

Next, subsection (4) was added. It reads

Section 6. (4) Subsections (2) and (3) do not preclude any law, program or activity that has as its object the amelioration in a province of conditions of individuals in that province who are socially or economically disadvantaged if the rate of employment in that province is below the rate of employment in Canada.

This subsection qualifies pure mobility even further: Any province that has a rate of employment below the national average may set up an affirmative action program designed to ameliorate the "conditions of individuals in that province who are socially or economically disadvantaged." In fact, this allows provinces with high unemployment to ignore the provisions of paragraph 2(b), which says anyone can work in any province.

Various interest groups in Canada remain unsatisfied with the final wording of the Constitution's guarantee of mobility rights. Those representing the poor, natives, homosexuals and other minorities that traditionally find it difficult to gain employment feel greater protection for them should have been built into section 6. A number of government representatives, notably from Nova Scotia, Newfoundland, the Yukon and the Northwest Territories also wanted more protection. Generally, they favour greater provincial or territorial control over hiring practices so that when job opportunities do arise in depressed areas those opportunities will go to long-term local residents. Northerners, especially, dislike the notion of unrestricted labour movement. They believe that when mega-projects like pipeline construction create jobs in the north, hiring priority should be given to long-time northern residents even if those residents require training. In contrast, the Canadian Chamber of Commerce wanted greater mobility and argued unsuccessfully to have the clause guaranteeing the free flow of people expanded to include the free flow of goods, services and capital.

Unlike so many other clauses in the Charter, mobility rights are not expected to be the subject of a great deal of litigation. The provinces won enough concessions to make the two remaining guarantees of free movement and access to work acceptable. However, undoubtedly there will be occasions when provincial or even federal economic development schemes are challenged because in someone's view they offend the spirit of mobility.

Legal Rights

> Section 7. Everyone has the right to life, liberty and security of
> the person and the right not to be deprived thereof except in
> accordance with the principles of fundamental justice.

In a democracy like Canada the rights to life, liberty and security of
person tend to be taken for granted. They seem to be such fundamental guarantees that the idea of their sparking serious controversy is
difficult to imagine. In fact, the potential for controversy is probably
greater here than in any other section of the Charter. The emotionally
charged abortion issue may well be fought over the first six words of
section 7: "Everyone has the right to life . . ."

The issues are obvious. They boil down to the two most fundamental questions in the abortion debate. When does an embryo or fetus
begin to live and when is an embryo or fetus brought within the
definition of "everyone?"

Almost every individual or group that submitted recommendations
to Parliament on this section found it too vague and too vulnerable to
wrong-minded interpretation by the courts. Antiabortionists wanted
rights for the unborn spelled out. They recommended wording like this:

> Everyone from the moment of conception onward who is inno-
> cent of a crime, has the absolute right to life.

That wording would prevent abortion but allow for the death penalty.
Proabortionists or "prochoice" groups also called for clarification. This
wording is typical of their recommendations:

> Nothing in this Charter is intended to extend rights to the embryo
> or fetus, nor to restrict in any manner the right of a woman to a
> medically safe abortion.

With opinion so completely divided on the right to life issue there
can be little doubt that this section will be among the first to be judicially
tested. In the United States a similar clause has been interpreted to
exclude the unborn from its protection, but American precedents,
though relevant, will not be binding on any Canadian court, certainly
not on our High Court. Moreover, even if the Supreme Court were to
follow the American lead and rule that the words "everyone" and "life"
offer no protection to the unborn, Parliament could still protect the
unborn by amending the Criminal Code. Such statutory protection

would not be as strong or as permanent as constitutional enshrinement because it could be changed by Parliament at any time.

The other elements of section 7 have attracted far less attention than the first six words. Several interest groups feel the expression "fundamental justice" is not specific enough and fear that it could be badly interpreted in a court challenge. Other groups wanted the right "to own property" added to this section. They feel that property rights are absolutely fundamental to the common law system of justice, which includes the notion "a man's home is his castle." The right to own property was deleted from the final draft at the insistence of the New Democratic party, which feared that such a concept would restrict the government's power to introduce equitable social democratic policies.

> Section 8. Everyone has the right to be secure against unreasonable search or seizure.
> Section 9. Everyone has the right not to be arbitrarily detained or imprisoned.

Sections 8 and 9 appear to protect Canadians by restricting police searches, seizures and detainments and by giving judges wide discretionary powers to declare such activities "unreasonable" or "arbitrary." On the other hand, what appear to be protections may end up being just the opposite: Police officers could end up with more power than they now have. The reason for this uncertainty is that no one can predict precisely how the courts will use their discretion. Unless no other logical conclusion is possible, no judge is bound to interpret sections 8 and 9 in the way the drafters may have intended.

Will the rules for search, seizure and arrest that are currently set out in the Criminal Code be accepted as binding or will judges be able to dismiss these rules as unreasonable in certain cases? Is it unreasonable for the police to search a home when the owner is away? Should the police always have a warrant or could situations arise where breaking into a home or office would be reasonable in a judge's mind? Can the police rip open furniture in search of illicit drugs? Can they seize business records or personal correspondence without explanation? Are skin searches, internal examinations, blood tests or breath tests reasonable ways to collect evidence? The answers to these questions and a hundred variations on them really depend on what judges and, ultimately, the Supreme Court think is "unreasonable" or "arbitrary" in relation to a given set of facts.

> Section 10. Everyone has the right on arrest or detention

(a) to be informed promptly of the reasons therefor;
(b) to retain and instruct counsel without delay and to be informed of that right; and
(c) to have the validity of the detention determined by way of *habeas corpus* and to be released if the detention is not lawful.

The vast majority of Canadians never get into trouble with the law, certainly not the sort of trouble that calls for lawyers and possible imprisonment. It often comes as a shock to them, then, to learn that the sort of restraints placed on American police officers, the sort of rules that American crime movies and television series have made so familiar to us, did not exist in Canada before the Constitution Act 1982 was proclaimed law.

Before the Charter became law, police did not carry a small card bearing a list of constitutional rights that had to be read to all suspected lawbreakers. The "right" to a lawyer existed in Canada, but it was not constitutionally guaranteed. Police were under no obligation to allow a suspected criminal to contact a lawyer immediately upon detainment. Regularly, suspects were held for hours, questioned and encouraged to incriminate themselves before they were allowed to make "that one phone call" that the American entertainment industry continually declares we all have the right to make.

The question is how close to the American practices has section 10 moved Canada? Clearly, the two situations will not be identical. For example, the right to remain silent upon arrest, a luxury Americans now enjoy, is notably absent from section 10. As well, until the courts interpret the words "promptly" and "without delay" in paragraphs (a) and (b) it is impossible to say exactly what new fetters the section has placed on police conduct.

The Canadian Association of Chiefs of Police and the Canadian Association of Crown Counsels both feel that a suspect's right to be promptly informed of the reasons for arrest (paragraph (a)) places an impossible burden on police officers. They point to the incredible complexity of the Criminal Code, especially in the areas of attempted crimes and conspiracies to commit crimes. Often, they say, it is simply impossible to tell an apprehended suspect exactly what charge he or she will ultimately be facing. The police and prosecutors fear that criminals may escape conviction on the grounds that they were not "promptly" told what they were being arrested for and thus were not given a fair opportunity to defend themselves. The chiefs of police and crown counsels asked Parliament to substitute the words "as soon as practicable" for "promptly." The request was denied.

It was denied largely because the word "promptly" was regarded by parliamentarians as a compromise. Police chiefs and crown counsels were not the only groups applying pressure to have this section amended. On the opposite side of the case, arguing for even tighter controls on police, were many civil rights advocates. Groups such as the Canadian Federation of Civil Liberties and Human Rights Association feel "promptly" is not fast enough. They suggested the word "immediately."

Interest groups on both sides seem satisfied with paragraph (b), the right to retain and instruct counsel, though there is generally a feeling that the words "without delay" will have to be defined on a case-by-case basis. Clearly, "without delay" will mean different things to a person arrested in the high Arctic than it will to someone picked up in downtown Halifax or Regina. One aspect of the right to retain counsel bothers some of the representatives of poor Canadians. Groups such as the Public Interest Advocacy Centre and the National Anti-Poverty Organization feel that the right to legal aid or some other form of government-funded counsel should have been included. The final wording, they say, makes the right to a lawyer a rich person's right only.

> Section 11. Any person charged with an offence has the right
>> (a) to be informed without unreasonable delay of the specific offence;
>> (b) to be tried within a reasonable time;

This section contains seven more paragraphs (c to i), which are reproduced at the end of this book. They spell out guarantees such as the presumption of innocence until proven guilty, the right to bail, the right to a jury trial for serious offences, protection against double jeopardy, and the right to lesser penalties in certain circumstances.

The first two paragraphs are reproduced here because they present the same question so many other guarantees in the Charter do—what exactly do they mean? Until "unreasonable" and "reasonable" are defined in the courts it will be impossible to say just what a person's rights are.

Another question arises about the possibility of conflict between paragraph 11(a) and paragraph 10(a). What happens if upon arrest a suspect is promptly informed of "the reasons therefor" (paragraph

10(a)) but is later charged with an unrelated or distantly related crime and so informed under paragraph 11(a)? Will the initial error so violate the suspect's rights as to destroy the crown's entire case? Or, in some situations, will information supplied when the formal charge is laid correct the situation?

It is this very sort of problem that has Canadian police officers and crown attorneys worried. They see the Charter as a breeding ground for the "technical defence," the sort of situation so prevalent in the United States, where an otherwise guilty person is set free because of a minor rights violation.

> Section 12. Everyone has the right not to be subjected to any cruel and unusual treatment or punishment.

The constitutional enshrinement of the notion that "cruel and unusual" punishment is unacceptable in a democratic society poses two questions for the future. The first deals with the treatment and punishment of criminals, especially those whose crimes make normal punishments inappropriate, the second with the propriety of capital punishment.

The words "cruel and unusual" are given a stature by being in the Constitution that they never before enjoyed. They invite lawyers to make submissions to judges on the types of sentences passed on convicted persons, and they also invite lawyers to challenge sentences already handed down. For example, judicial notice has been taken of the fact that certain types of criminals, especially child molesters, are harshly treated by their fellow inmates in prison. There are many documented cases of violent beatings and even murders of imprisoned child molesters. Is it cruel and unusual to place a convicted child molester in prison if there is a strong likelihood that he will not survive the sentence? The question is certain to be posed and answered in the courts.

Capital punishment is not an immediate issue because it was abolished in Canada in 1976. However, many people across the country support the reinstatement of the death penalty. In 1981 the Progressive Conservative opposition in Parliament dedicated one of its allotted days (days reserved for debate on subjects chosen by opposition parties) to debating a motion to reopen the issue by placing it before a parliamentary committee. The motion was defeated, but the death penalty issue is still very much alive. If the death penalty were reinstated, it would almost certainly be challenged under section 12 as "cruel and unusual." The success of any challenge would depend, in part, on whether or not the challengers could find a way to counteract the considerable body of jurisprudence to the effect that capital punishment is not cruel and unusual.

Although section 12 is certain to be used by defence lawyers who wish to alter sentences and by opponents of capital punishment, the drafters of the section did not see it as an invitation to sweeping change. During the debate that preceded adoption by Parliament of the Charter, the government described section 12 as a "neutral" clause. The belief is that by using the words "cruel" and "unusual" together their effect on the present approach to punishing criminals in Canada is negated. The reasoning goes like this: If viewed in isolation, any form of punishment is cruel, but section 12 does not use the word "cruel" in isolation. It combines it with "unusual," and in the federal government's opinion, no form of punishment now employed in Canada can be said to be unusual.

> Section 13. A witness who testifies in any proceedings has the right not to have any incriminating evidence so given used to incriminate that witness in any other proceedings, except in a prosecution for perjury or for the giving of contradictory evidence.
> Section 14. A party or witness in any proceedings who does not understand or speak the language in which the proceedings are conducted or who is deaf has the right to the assistance of an interpreter.

Sections 13 and 14 are intended to guarantee that no pertinent testimony is lost to a court because the only person capable of giving it is either afraid or incapable of doing so. The latter section is clear; it merely guarantees foreign-language-speakers and deaf persons the professional assistance they require to make themselves understood. Section 13 embodies a more complicated guarantee. It streamlines those provisions of the federal and provincial Evidence Acts that allow someone to give testimony incriminating him or herself in a crime without fear of being convicted on the strength of that testimony.

For example, suppose X is being tried for murder. His defense is that he could not have done it because at the time of the killing he was robbing a bank in another town with his friend Y. In order to prove innocence, both X and Y could admit to the robbery without fear of prosecution. Their testimony would obviously encourage the police to investigate their involvement in the robbery, but no charge could be laid solely on the strength of the alibi to the murder charge. Under the old Evidence Act, protection from prosecution had to be claimed before incriminating testimony was given or it did not apply. Under section 13 the protection applies automatically.

Equality Rights

> Section 15. (1) Every individual is equal before and under the law and has the right to the equal protection and equal benefit of the law without discrimination and, in particular, without discrimination based on race, national or ethnic origin, colour, religion, sex, age or mental or physical disability.

The simple existence of section 15 is a monument to the power of persistence and popular will. The federal government argued tirelessly for an equality or nondiscrimination statement in the Constitution and its efforts were furthered by dozens of individuals and interest groups. Many of Canada's premiers would have preferred to leave out equality rights altogether. Their feeling was that such rights are best protected by provincial human rights laws, laws that are more easily changed than the Constitution and, therefore, best able to adapt to changing views.

Even among those who lobbied for the constitutional enshrinement of equality rights, there was considerable disagreement on just what protections should be included. Race, national or ethnic origin, colour and religion seemed to be acceptable to all, but the inclusion of sex, age and mental or physical disability was not universally applauded. A lengthy and often acrimonious debate on just how broad these last three guarantees should be continued right up until 8 December 1981 when the resolution respecting the new Constitution was finally adopted by the Senate. Women, pensioners, children's rights advocates, spokespersons for the disabled and dozens of other organizations and individuals lobbied intensely in an effort to force amendments. In the end, some interest groups were justly pleased with their accomplishments, others were disappointed. Still others were confused as to exactly what their status was.

The demands made by those who sought an expanded nondiscrimination section and the doubts expressed by those who opposed it offer the best glimpse of what impact the final wording of subsection 15(1) may have on Canadian life. The protection against discrimination based on race, national or ethnic origin, colour and religion is not examined here. It breaks no new ground in human rights legislation. The last three categories, however—sex, age and mental or physical disability—raise unique issues.

SEXUAL EQUALITY

Women's Rights

The battle for enshrinement of equal rights for women was characterized by dramatic reversals, crushing disappointment and ultimate
success. In the initial version of the Charter, introduced in the House of
Commons in October 1980, women's rights were only partially guaranteed. After much debate that guarantee of equality was made absolute,
only to be cut back again in November 1981 at the insistence of several
of the premiers. Last minute demonstrations and lobbying resulted in
the reinstatement of the stronger protection with one condition. Equality Rights are one of the categories of rights and freedoms that can be
avoided by notwithstanding legislation passed according to the exception provisions in section 33.

The original version of subsection 15(1) omitted the words "and
under the law." The section merely said "Everyone has the right to
equality before the law . . ." The difference may seem minor; it is not.
Women's groups, such as the Canadian Advisory Council on the
Status of Women, presented extremely detailed briefs that proved
conclusively that "equality before the law" is no guarantee of equality
at all. That very wording is in the John Diefenbaker Bill of Rights, and
the courts have interpreted it very narrowly. Equality before the law
only guarantees equal *access* to the courts; it does not prohibit
discriminatory laws.

Women's groups also found the negative nature of subsection
15(1) disturbing. They felt it had a prohibitory tone in that despite its
guarantee of equality what it really does is prohibit discrimination. They
lobbied Parliament for a separate clause recognizing women's rights, a
strong positive affirmation of the equality of sexes. The women won
both their battles. Subsection 15(1) was reworded "before and under
the law," and a new section, 28, was added clearly stating that the
rights and freedoms referred to in the Charter "are guaranteed equally
male and female persons."

Women were overjoyed but the joy soon died. When the Supreme
Court ruled on 28 September 1981 that the federal government could
not properly ask Britain to amend and send home the Constitution
without provincial consent, the prime minister agreed to another first
ministers conference to see if a consensus could be worked out. The
conference was held in early November and an agreement was
reached, but that agreement dealt women a hard blow. Both the
positive statement of equality contained in section 28 and subsection

15(1) were weakened by being placed in that class of rights that can be avoided under the notwithstanding provisions of section 33.

Women's groups across the country rallied. They held demonstrations, petitioned provincial governments and kept the pressure on in Ottawa. This time, their efforts won only a part of what they sought. At the eleventh hour, section 28 was removed from the category of rights that can be avoided by notwithstanding legislation, but subsection 15(1) was not.

Despite the possibility of notwithstanding laws being passed under the exception provisions of section 33, women hailed the final draft of the new Constitution as a victory. The general feeling among them appears to be this: They must remain vigilant but political reality (women make up half the voters) would make it foolhardy for any government to use the notwithstanding power to limit women's rights.

Homosexuals' Rights

The Charter does not provide homosexuals with unequivocal protection. Subsection 15(1) does prohibit discrimination on grounds of sex, but there is considerable jurisprudence to the effect that the word "sex" describes only males and females and has nothing to do with sexual preference. Organizations such as the Canadian Association of Lesbians and Gay Men contend that this interpretation is archaic and should be replaced by one that recognizes sexual preference. Homosexuals argue that the basic guarantee of equality in subsection 15(1) should not be accompanied by a list of protected classes of persons. They say that by their very nature such lists encourage discrimination against any class of persons not included. A real equality guarantee, argue homosexual rights advocates, would simply prohibit discrimination, period.

Some groups adamantly oppose constitutional guarantees for homosexuals. The Church of Jesus Christ of Latter Day Saints, for example, contends that broadly stated nondiscrimination rights of the type proposed by homosexuals would legitimate homosexual marriages, unions to which the church is totally opposed.

Without question, the intent of the "sex" protection in subsection 15(1) will be debated by both sides of the issue in a future court challenge and pressure from both sides will continue to be felt by Canada's lawmakers. However, unless the political and moral climate changes dramatically and the Supreme Court takes a far different view of the word "sex" than is now the usual one, it seems unlikely that subsection 15(1) will be interpreted as a protection for homosexuals.

AGE: EQUALITY FOR YOUNG AND OLD

Section 1 of the Diefenbaker Bill of Rights (much of which is carried forward into the Charter of Rights and Freedoms) formed the basis of the original draft of subsection 15(1). That draft was altered to correct the general flaw pointed out by women's groups and to include the handicapped. Both changes were the result of considerable lobbying, but two other changes were made without any prompting or lobbying whatsoever. Two categories not included in Diefenbaker's Bill were added. Under the Charter discrimination is prohibited on grounds of ethnic origin or age. The former, ethnic origin, hardly requires elucidation, but the inclusion of "age" raises some interesting possibilities.

Society tends to classify people in accordance with the number of years they have spent on this earth. It matters not in most cases whether the classifications are reasonable in particular circumstances; generally, they are inflexible. So, a sickly and weak five year old may begin school, while a large healthy four year old may not. At sixty-five a person must stop working even if he or she wishes to continue, is able to do so and needs the money. Once classified as a senior citizen one may take advantage of a number of price reductions (in the cost of movies, for example, or public transit fares) even if one is rich. Junior sports tournaments are divided into age brackets; certain university courses will accept no entrants above a particular age. Voting, drinking, enlisting, marrying, adopting, all these are available to some but not to others. The test is age.

Which, if any, of these age-related restrictions will survive the prohibition against age discrimination in the new Constitution? Certain of them are bound to be regarded as necessary by lawmakers and thus made exempt from the effects of the Charter by notwithstanding legislation passed under section 33. But no government is likely to go through the tedious process of enacting a separate law to preserve each and every existing age requirement simply to maintain the status quo. Political fallout aside, such an undertaking would tie up a legislative assembly for years.

Parliament and all provincial legislatures are likely to pass notwithstanding legislation that allows some form of forced retirement. The same will also probably be done for drinking, voting, marrying and enlisting regulations and for laws intended to protect the public, such as age requirements for various types of licences. Beyond these, speculation becomes difficult. One might expect the courts to apply some sort of "reasonable" test to many age requirements, ruling, for example, that a fifty-year-old applicant to medical school could "reasonably" be denied entry on the basis of age, all apparent constitutional protection aside. But there is no specific "reasonable" requirement in subsection 15(1) and the courts may feel that the general power of governments to limit the Charter's protections (section 1) is not broad enough to justify all of the discriminatory practices based on age that are now contained in federal and provincial laws. Certainly, lesser regulatory bodies, such as municipalities and institutions, will be hard-pressed to bring their restrictive age requirements within the limitation guidelines in section 1.

What seems probable is that along with many nonsensical age discriminations, reasonable ones may fall as well. The advantages that are often bestowed on senior citizens may be challenged by younger people not entitled to them and lost. Special rates and regulations for children may be abolished as well. It is certain that women will not tolerate any form of discrimination, nor will different racial groups or different religious organizations. Unless the courts develop a double standard, something that is not anticipated in subsection 15(1), it is fair to assume that the age protection will be as strictly policed by the courts as all the others.

MENTAL OR PHYSICAL DISABILITY

There were no protections whatsoever for the handicapped in the first version of the new Constitution, the one placed before Parliament in the fall of 1980. The Canadian Human Rights Commission and a number of other human rights advocates pressed Parliament to expand subsection 15(1) to include mentally and physically disabled persons. Demonstrators with white canes, seeing-eye dogs, wheelchairs and placards demanding equality became a familiar sight on Parliament Hill. As they did in the case of women, federal parliamentarians responded. Subsection 15(1) was expanded and the handicapped are now guaranteed equality subject only to section 33 and its provisions for notwithstanding legislation.

There was a considerable amount of opposition to the inclusion of equality for the mentally and physically disabled. Many politicians fear that rights for the handicapped, if carried to their logical conclusion, could create economic chaos. They fear that radical equality advocates may pressure the courts for declarations that "equality" means true unconditional equality in all things. That, say those opposed to rights for the handicapped, could be the most expensive exercise in civil rights ever undertaken.

These are some of the examples suggested: If the courts interpret "equality" broadly enough, bus lines, airlines, taxis, trains and all other modes of public transportation would have to be redesigned and rebuilt to admit wheelchairs, seeing-eye dogs and any other apparatus deemed necessary by handicapped individuals. Public buildings would have to provide far more assistance than a few ramps at the doors and a few handrails in the washrooms. Paper currency would have to be sized differently or imprinted with braille insignia for blind people. The list is not a short one and every item would be expensive. The cost may be nothing compared to the indignities and frustrations suffered each day by disabled Canadians, but it may come as a shock to any taxpayer who thought equality for the handicapped merely meant a change of attitude.

OTHERS

Those left out of the protected list in subsection 15(1) or not mentioned specifically in separate Charter provisions are not necessarily without guarantees of rights under the new Constitution. Subsection 15(1) is not merely a list of protected classes of persons. It also begins with a general protection that reads "Every individual is equal before and under the law and has the right to the equal protection and equal benefit of the law without discrimination . . ." Judges are free to interpret this phrase broadly, perhaps to include other classes of persons not mentioned specifically.

Such a judicial approach, however, would be out of keeping with the way Canadian courts have traditionally dealt with nondiscrimination laws. In clauses such as 15(1) where a general statement of principle is followed by a specific list, courts have generally regarded the list as exhaustive in the sense that they have not employed the general provision as a way to add specific new classes. Still, the choice lies with the courts. Until at least one case goes as far as the Supreme Court, it is not possible to say absolutely that the normal tradition of strict interpretation will be followed.

There is another section, 26, that may contain hidden protections for individuals not included elsewhere in the Charter. It states

Section 26. The guarantee in this Charter of certain rights and freedoms shall not be construed as denying the existence of any other rights and freedoms that exist in Canada.

The question is, what exactly does section 26 mean? The answer may be a long time in coming. Under the old Constitution most rights and freedoms were not guaranteed in writing, but many did exist. Over the years since Confederation some were identified and protected by the courts. Others were never the subject of judicial scrutiny, but that fact does not negate the possibility that they exist. Rights for the unborn or expanded native rights are typical of the sort of issues that could find their way before the courts through a section 26 challenge. For example, if antiabortionists can convince the courts that rights for the unborn were a part of the old unwritten Constitution, then those rights will effectively be guaranteed by section 26.

The history of the jurisprudence in the area of unwritten constitutional rights in Canada indicates that only very fundamental matters fall into the category of existing but unspecified rights. Freedom of discussion and freedom of religion are two examples. Still, it cannot be said absolutely that the courts will not recognize and protect other rights and freedoms under the terms of section 26.

AFFIRMATIVE ACTION

> Section 15.(2) Subsection (1) does not preclude any law, program or activity that has as its object the amelioration of conditions of disadvantaged individuals or groups including those that are disadvantaged because of race, national or ethnic origin, colour, religion, sex, age or mental or physical disability.

This is the second affirmative action clause in the new Charter of Rights and Freedoms. The first allowed provinces with high unemployment rates to pass laws giving hiring preference to resident job seekers. The affirmative action programs envisaged under subsection 15(2) are far broader in scope.

Affirmative action is a euphemism for legal discrimination. The idea is based on the belief that certain groups or minorities have historically received fewer opportunities in society than have members of society's majority. The example most often cited in North America is the treatment of blacks in the United States. The first step in reversing discrimination against minorities is to outlaw it. However, because guarantees of equality are often an insufficient cure for years of discrimination, affirmative action programs are created. In an effort to quickly improve the status of aggrieved minority groups, the state establishes programs that discriminate in the minority's favour: Admissions standards are lowered at universities; hiring procedures are changed to favour minorities; government grants or tax credits are offered as incentives for companies to hire or train members of selected minorities.

In the United States the concept of equality is built into the Constitution, but affirmative action is not. Because of this the United States Supreme Court has ruled that affirmative action programs, while laudable in their goals, cannot be so constructed or administered as to discriminate against members of the majority. This ruling was handed down in the famous Bakke Case.* Bakke complained to the court that he had been denied admission to medical school not because he was unqualified but because the school he had applied to had adopted an affirmative action program. The program reserved a number of places in medical school for minority group members, even though the minority applicants might not have qualifications equal to white student applicants. The court agreed with Bakke's view that though blacks and other minority groups should be helped such assistance should not block the valid ambitions of the majority. The school was ordered to admit Bakke.

Subsection 15(2) will effectively preclude Canadians from challenging affirmative action programs in the same way Bakke did in the United States. Such programs are not a new idea in Canada. The Canadian Human Rights Act, for example, makes provisions for similar remedial programs and even goes so far as to give the federal government the right to force such programs on persons or institutions that have been found to be discriminating against members of minority groups.

EQUALITY RIGHTS ENACTED

Although section 15 is part of the new Constitution, its provisions will not come into force until 17 April 1985, three years after the new Constitution became law. This delay, which is stipulated in subsection 32(2) of the Charter, is intended to give federal and provincial officials adequate time to prepare for the wide-sweeping changes subsection 15(1) will bring. Every law will be examined during those three years in an effort to determine whether or not any provision of it violates the nondiscrimination principles in 15(1). Once a list of offending laws is compiled, federal and provincial governments will have to decide whether to amend the laws, pass notwithstanding exceptions to protect certain discriminatory practices or simply let the offending laws stand and wait for the courts to declare them invalid.

---

*The Regents of the University of California v. Bakke (1978) 438 U.S. 265.

Official Languages of Canada

With the exception of making New Brunswick a completely bilingual province, the sections of the Constitution that pertain to official languages contain little that is new. Essentially, they adopt the language guarantees that existed in the old Constitution and enshrine the equal status of English and French at the federal level. Official language guarantees are set out in section 16–22, which are reproduced at the end of this book.

New Brunswick is now officially a bilingual province by its own choice. Its Premier Richard Hatfield recommended the change, which was later ratified by a vote of the province's legislature. Like New Brunswick, Ontario has a large population of residents whose first language is French and a considerable amount of pressure was brought to bear on Ontario Premier William Davis to follow Hatfield's lead. Davis declined to do so.

Although Canadians outside New Brunswick will notice little change in the bilingual nature of the country, the official language sections of the Charter do alter the status of the concept of bilingualism in Canada. Formerly, bilingualism at the federal level was largely guaranteed by the Official Languages Act, a mere federal statute that could be amended or even repealed at any time. Now, any weakening of the official language guarantees would require a constitutional amendment, a far more difficult process than passing federal legislation.

Minority Language Educational Rights

Minority language educational rights are set out in section 23 of the Charter, which does two things. First, it provides a number of rules governing who may have access to education in English or French when the language preferred is not the language of the majority. Second, it establishes general guidelines to assist provincial governments in determining just what educational facilities they must provide for linguistic minority groups. As well, there are special provisions governing the language of education in Quebec.

Three points are essential to an understanding of how this section will work. First, only Canadian citizens have a right to demand minority language educational facilities. Provinces may choose to extend this right to landed immigrants or visitors, but the Constitution does not require them to do so. Second, all of the citizens' rights are conditional on vague numbers tests: No matter how strong a citizen's claim for

English or French language education, it will fail unless the location where the claim is made has a minority language population that is large enough. Finally, only English and French minority groups have minority language educational rights. No other language group, no matter how large, has a constitutional right to be educated in its mother tongue. As well, even the rights for qualified minorities extend only as far as secondary education. There are no provisions for minority language education beyond high school.

Which citizens, then, may demand an English or French education for their children? According to the Charter, anyone who fits into one of the following three categories qualifies:

1. Citizens who form part of a French or English minority group and who first learned and still understand the language of that group
2. Citizens who attended either a French or English primary school in Canada and who now reside in a province where the language in which they were taught is the language of the minority population of the province
3. Citizens who have already educated or begun educating one child in French or English

These three groups have the right to have all of their children educated in the language of the English or French minority *where numbers warrant*.

What exactly is meant by "where numbers warrant" is unclear. The section merely sets out general guidelines for provincial governments to follow, guidelines that direct governments to increase the facilities available for French or English minority education as the size of the linguistic minority increases. No numbers, no ratios, no "bottom line" is established. Provinces are merely told that where numbers warrant facilities must be provided and as those numbers grow, so must the quality of the facilities.

CRITICISM OF SECTION 23

The new provisions for minority language educational rights have not been universally hailed. The major complaint is that they are not broad enough. Several individuals and interest groups feel that the only truly fair approach to language education is to guarantee simply and clearly complete freedom of choice. They contend that restricting choice to citizens or to locations where numbers warrant is a needless, even harmful, refinement. The Commissioner of Official Languages, Maxwell Yalden, the Council of Quebec Minorities, L'Association canadienne-français de l'Ontario, the Société franco-manitobaine and many more interest groups have all called for absolute free choice. Other criticisms have been less sweeping.

There is some concern over how and by whom testing will be done to determine whether or not an individual qualifies under one of the three tests in section 23. One subsection demands that a parent's "first language learned and still understood is that of the English or French linguistic minority population of the province in which they reside." How does one prove that someone who speaks French or English now in fact learned it as a second language? What do the words "still understood" mean? Under its language law, Bill 101, Quebec set up a bureaucracy charged with investigating demands for minority language education and testing the language capacity of citizens. It has not been a very popular experiment. Other provinces may find it less costly to offer complete freedom of choice rather than to try to set up a system of policing.

As well, some people have criticized the rather vague guidelines set out in "where numbers warrant" tests for government funding. The fear is that without a more specific criterion for action, uniformity of approach will be impossible. What Saskatchewan regards as a sufficiently large minority to warrant a special French language program, for example, may be viewed as insufficient in British Columbia. Or vice versa. The result would be great uncertainty in the minds of parents considering a move from one province to another. Unless provinces quickly adopt clear and unequivocal guidelines on their own, Canadians will have to wait for a court ruling on how the "where numbers warrant" tests are to be applied.

THE IMPACT OF SECTION 23

Nowhere have the provisions of section 23 had more impact than in Quebec. Government representatives there consider it to be a totally unacceptable infringement on an area of lawmaking that they have guarded jealously. Quebec's own language law, Bill 101, contains a number of complicated rules and regulations that stipulate who may be educated in English. Section 23 renders many of these rules and regulations inoperative.

In order to defuse the political bomb that Quebec's Parti Québécois government threatened to create out of section 23, a later provision, section 59, was included. The idea was to reduce the impact of the minority language educational provisions in Quebec by allowing that province to phase in part of the new regulations according to its own timetable. Section 59 states that paragraph 23(1)(a), which grants inviolate minority language educational rights to every Canadian whose mother tongue is one of the official languages, will not come into effect in Quebec unless that province's legislature authorizes it.

Until the language provisions are tested in the courts, it is almost impossible to estimate what effect this partial exemption will have in Quebec. The exemption in section 59 only applies to one of the three categories of Canadians who now have the right to demand minority language education for their children. Thus, even if Quebec never moves under section 59, two categories of citizens will be able to demand an English education based on the provisions of section 23 that are not affected by the exemption. Parents who themselves received primary education in English or who have begun educating one or more of their children in English may move to Quebec and (where numbers warrant) demand an English education for all their children. That was certainly not the case under Bill 101. It appears that section 59 merely gives Quebec the power to refuse demands for English education to children of a very small group of individuals: English Quebecers who were educated in French and who had previously educated none of their children in English.

Because bilingualism has traditionally been an emotional issue, the fact that the minority language educational provisions are in the Constitution at all is regarded by many as a genuine triumph. For the first time Canadians who relocate in the country will have a good chance of being assured the choice of either French or English educational facilities. Although this choice already exists in some places, it exists at the pleasure of the government. From now on, where the guidelines in section 23 are met, the choice will be constitutionally guaranteed.

Enforcement of Rights and Freedoms

Section 24.(1) Anyone whose rights or freedoms, as guaranteed by this Charter, have been infringed or denied may apply to a court of competent jurisdiction to obtain such remedy as the court considers appropriate and just in the circumstances.

The objective of this section appears to be commendable, the process reasonable. Clearly if Canadians are promised inalienable rights and freedoms they must have some remedy available to them should those rights and freedoms be denied or diminished. Where better to turn for assistance than the courts? Despite its apparent reasonableness, however, this section has drawn a steady flow of criticism ever since it was proposed. Most of the criticism has come from those responsible for maintaining law and order in Canada—the police and crown attorneys. Some of them genuinely fear that this section is too vague. It appears to give unlimited power to Canada's judges.

Typical of the complaints levelled against the Charter's enforcement section is this paragraph from a piece entitled "Crime and the Proposed Constitution," which was written in 1981 by Brockville, Ontario Assistant Crown Attorney Douglas Mackintosh for the information of his fellow crown attorneys.

> Section 24 seems to be typical of the present approach by the government to constitutional amendments. It is the most astonishing section of law ever to be proposed in Canada. It is like an irrevocable bearer's cheque made out to the courts with the amount of power left blank to be filled out as they please. ". . . such remedy as the court considers appropriate" is the cudgel provided. In itself this section, carrying as it does unlimited penalty, could be more powerful than the whole of the criminal code, and it could easily throw the whole question of the independence of the judiciary into doubt. And since it is more powerful than the criminal code, it could lead to the abandoning of the criminal code and a whole new approach to crime through civil liberties.

Mr. Mackintosh and those who share his concerns contend that though section 24 was designed to provide relief for law-abiding citizens whose rights have been infringed upon (and may in some instances do so) more often it will furnish criminals not only with a method of "beating the rap" on a technicality but also with a means of tormenting the very police officers who try to further the cause of justice by bringing the offenders to court. Those opposed to the enforcement provision of the Charter paint a picture of criminals suing the police on a regular basis. These suits would be based on technical complaints arising out of alleged violations of sections 7–14 of the Charter (under the heading of Legal Rights). The criminals could demand everything from an apology to monetary damages as compensation for infringement on their rights.

Such fears as Mr. Mackintosh raises cannot be dismissed out of hand. However, those fears are largely based on the supposition that the courts will interpret the words "such remedy as the court considers appropriate" in such a way as to severely hamstring police activity. Although this *could* happen, the Canadian experience thus far has not been characterized by the sort of adversarial relation between law enforcers and the courts that would create the situation envisaged by Mr. Mackintosh and his adherents. Moreover, the section states that the courts must be "just" in these cases. Justice, thus far in Canada, has never been such a one-sided affair.

> Section 24.(2) Where, in proceedings under subsection (1), a court concludes that evidence was obtained in a manner that infringed or denied any rights or freedoms guaranteed by this Charter, the evidence shall be excluded if it is established that, having regard to all the circumstances, the admission of it in the proceedings would bring the administration of justice into disrepute.

The intent here is clearly to encourage police officers to do their work and gather their evidence within the guidelines set out in the Legal Rights part of the Charter (sections 7–14). The price paid for not doing so might be a ruling from the bench that some piece of evidence gathered in violation of one or another enshrined legal right could not be used against the person charged.

The inadmissability of improperly obtained evidence is not a new concept in Canadian criminal law. Such evidence as a confession beaten out of a suspect has always been held to be inadmissable at trial. The traditional test for the determination of admissability of a confession is two-fold: The judge at trial must determine whether a confession is voluntary, then the jury must decide whether the confession is true. Even if the judge decides that the accused confessed of his own free will it is still open to the jury to decide that, though voluntary, the confession is a lie. It is possible, then, for an accused to convince a jury that for whatever reason—emotional instability, desire for recognition or plain foolhardiness—he confessed, to a crime he did not, in fact, commit. Such a defence would only succeed where the confession was the sole piece of evidence pointing towards guilt.

In a typical trial, however, confessions very rarely stand alone. Generally there is other evidence—witnesses, a motive, a weapon—linking the accused to the crime. In these situations the admissability rules change dramatically. In Canada, the Supreme Court has ruled that even though involuntary confessions are themselves inadmissable, evidence found as a result of such confessions will be admitted.

The Court made this ruling in 1970 in a case called *The Queen* v. *Wray*. Wray was the prime suspect in a murder investigation. The police interrogated him rather forcefully and under the pressure Wray broke down. He signed a statement saying where he had hidden the murder weapon and subsequently led the police to the swamp where the weapon, a rifle, was concealed. Both the trial judge and the Ontario court of appeal rejected the statement as involuntary. According to the appeal court, such tactics for forcing confessions out of people were unfair and "brought the administration of justice into disrepute." The High Court rejected the concept of fairness completely. Where evidence is true and relevant, ruled the Court, the trial judge has no discretion to exclude it simply because it was improperly obtained. As Mr. Justice Judson said, "There is no judicial discretion permitting the exclusion of relevant evidence, in this case highly relevant evidence, on the ground of unfairness to the accused."

That was the law in 1970. That was the law under the old Constitution. What is the law now? Crown attorneys like Douglas Mackintosh believe subsection 24(2) will nullify the rule in the *Wray* case. They envisage a new situation entirely, in which police will be incapable of carrying out investigations without violating a suspect's rights and thus rendering evidence obtained inadmissable. They paint an American picture of every second accused "beating the rap" because a clever lawyer has been able to use the Constitution to have some vital piece of incriminating evidence excluded from the jury. They warn that the cost of police work will skyrocket as investigating officers, unwilling to risk getting a statement, will instead turn to wiretapping, lengthy searches and fingerprinting in their search for evidence.

Many of Canada's defence lawyers agree with the crown attorneys that subsection 24(2) may cause more problems than it solves but, as one might suspect, the defence bar sees different problems. They disagree that forcing police to be fair in seeking confessions will mean fewer statements and fewer convictions. In the United States, they say, the statistics simply do not bear out this thesis. What defence lawyers fear is that police will use subsection 24(2) as an excuse to demand more wiretaps, more search warrants, more access generally to draconian investigative methods. As Toronto criminal lawyer Edward Greenspan put it during an address to a criminal law symposium in Ottawa, "The end result of the Charter of Rights is that we will be worse off. They [the police] will do everything now. They'll go wild."

Perhaps more than with any other section of the Charter the real onus for protecting Canadians from abuses under subsection 24(2) will be on politicians, not judges. If the courts do interpret this subsection as a mandate to exclude evidence gained by improper police conduct, then the pressure on politicians to give the police more power may become incredible. Politicians will then be forced to determine the real intent and spirit of the Charter and to decide if that intent and spirit are compatible with the demands for an increase in police power.

Miscellaneous Provisions

MULTICULTURAL HERITAGE

> Section 27. This Charter shall be interpreted in a manner consistent with the preservation and enhancement of the multicultural heritage of Canadians.

The inclusion of this section represents a major achievement by Canada's ethnic and cultural organizations. The originally proposed Charter made no mention of multicultural heritage. A number of interest groups, including the Canadian Polish Congress and the Ukrainian Canadian Committee, found it objectionable that only persons of French and English origin were constitutionally recognized. These objections resulted in the inclusion of the above section.

This section does not confer any new rights on Canada's ethnic communities. It is intended to ensure that any interpretation of the Charter must meet the objective of preserving and enhancing the multicultural heritage of Canada, which was the policy of the federal government before the Charter was adopted. Any activity that can be seen as beneficial to any ethnic group is now constitutionally protected. For example, although English and French are the only official languages in the Constitution, the government may recognize the desires of some people to use other languages. Grants to Polish, Ukrainian, Italian or other ethnic cultural centres cannot be challenged as unconstitutional simply because only French and English have "official" status.

DENOMINATIONAL SCHOOLS

> Section 29. Nothing in this Charter abrogates or derogates from any rights or privileges guaranteed by or under the Constitution of Canada in respect of denominational, separate or dissentient schools.

Like so many other protections this one did not appear in the first draft of the Charter. It was included at the insistence of groups such as the Ontario Conference of Catholic Bishops and The Joint Executive of the Denominational Education Committee of Newfoundland. These groups and others with similar goals support the protection of individual rights and freedoms in the Charter, but they feared that as the courts later interpreted and strengthened individual rights the result might be an erosion of collective rights.

This section does not confer any new rights. It is intended to be a signal that the existing rights of denominational, separate or dissentient schools are protected at least as much as they were under the old Constitution.

RIGHTS OF THE ABORIGINAL PEOPLES OF CANADA

At first glance, the way aboriginal and treaty rights are included in the new Constitution is somewhat confusing. They appear to be recognized twice, once within the Charter in section 25, then a second time as a separate part immediately following the Charter, in section 35. The double entry, however, is perfectly logical in legal terms. The first clause, section 25, is designed to ensure that none of the rights given in the Charter infringe on aboriginal rights. The second clause, section 35, is positioned outside the Charter to emphasize the separate nature and special status of aboriginal rights.

This somewhat cumbersome approach to protecting and recognizing aboriginal rights reflects the uncertainty that surrounded the issue during the constitutional reform process. In the initial draft of the Charter, published in October 1980, native rights were mentioned only in passing. A general clause near the end of that first draft stated that the Charter was not intended to affect any rights or freedoms not specified in it "including any rights or freedoms that pertain to the native peoples of Canada."

Canada's native rights organizations condemned the phrase as completely inadequate. Like so many other interest groups in the country, the natives lobbied for clearer constitutional protection. The native people, however, were not seeking equality. They wanted quite the opposite—a clear statement in the new Constitution affirming that they are not equal, by means of a clause that recognized a special native status, one that set them apart from all other Canadians. Such a clause would have to spell out beyond any shadow of a doubt that aboriginal rights existed, were unique from all other human rights and could not be infringed upon or lessened by any other constitutional enactment.

As the Constitution was debated and studied by parliamentarians there was substantial support for the native people's position. However, even among supporters there was considerable uncertainty as well. Almost everyone wanted to do something more to guarantee aboriginal rights, but no one seemed to know for sure just what a stronger guarantee might produce. No one, it seemed, could define aboriginal rights and everyone possessed some degree of scepticism about the wisdom of guaranteeing an unknown commodity. Did aboriginal rights mean land claims, special hunting and fishing rights and exemptions from taxation and immigration regulations? There were many questions but few concrete answers. The native spokespeople did nothing to clear up the confusion because they preferred to have aboriginal rights recognized and guaranteed but not narrowly construed.

After months of discussion, members of Parliament came up with what they hoped would be an acceptable solution. Section 25 was added to the Charter as a defence against conflicting claims arising out of other Charter sections and section 34 (later renumbered 35) was placed after the Charter to emphasize the special status of aboriginal rights. This is how the two sections appeared in the draft of the proposed constitutional clauses that were approved by the House of Commons on 23 April 1981:

> Section 25. The guarantee in this Charter of certain rights and freedoms shall not be construed so as to abrogate or derogate from any aboriginal, treaty or other rights or freedoms that pertain to the aboriginal peoples of Canada including
> (a) any rights or freedoms that have been recognized by the Royal Proclamation of October 7, 1763; and
> (b) any rights or freedoms that may be acquired by the aboriginal peoples of Canada by way of land claims settlement.
> Section 34. (1) The aboriginal and treaty rights of the aboriginal peoples of Canada are hereby recognized and affirmed.
> (2) In this Act, "aboriginal peoples of Canada" includes the Indian, Inuit and Métis peoples of Canada.

To explain the intended effects of sections 25 and 34 it is perhaps easiest to rely on the "sword and shield" analogy so well known to lawyers who spend much of their time trying to understand the purpose of legislation of all kinds. The idea is that some laws are designed to protect, thus shields, others to carve out new rights, swords. Section 25 was intended to be a shield. It tells judges who may be confronted with the Charter in years to come that no matter what other sections of the Charter appear to say, no section is intended to limit any aboriginal rights that may exist in Canada. What section 25 does not say is that any aboriginal rights do in fact exist. That positive statement was left to section 34, the sword.

When the new sections were announced by Justice Minister Jean Chrétien native representatives were jubilant. It was a remarkable victory. Section 34 was not as strong a guarantee as many would have liked, but it was a guarantee, a positive statement affirming the exist- ence of aboriginal rights and special status for natives. The jubilation was short lived.

At the same November 1981 constitutional conference where women's rights were temporarily diminished in the search for federal- provincial consensus, section 34 was dropped. Too many premiers were alarmed by the vagueness of the concept of "aboriginal rights." They did not wish to enshrine in the Constitution a clause that might totally disrupt the status quo in their provinces.

As the women had done, the native people again set to work. They lobbied members of Parliament and of the provincial legislatures, they demonstrated and they even commenced legal action in Britain in an eleventh-hour effort to stop Westminster from amending the Constitu- tion and sending it home to Canada without stronger aboriginal rights guarantees. Finally, as they had in the case of women's rights, the premiers opposed to native rights guarantees capitulated. But not completely: Section 34 was restored to the Charter, but it was changed. The word "existing" was added. The section was also renumbered as 35 and now reads

Section 35. (1) The existing aboriginal and treaty rights of the aboriginal peoples of Canada are hereby recognized and affirmed.
(2) In this Act, "aboriginal peoples of Canada" includes the Indian, Inuit and Métis peoples of Canada.

It is impossible to predict exactly what effect, if any, the word "existing" will have on aboriginal rights. Some native representatives are convinced its inclusion will limit their rights to claims existing before the Constitution Act 1982 was adopted. They say aboriginal rights cannot be defined for good reason—they are in flux, constantly changing and developing. Any attempt to limit that development is unacceptable to many native groups. Native representatives are suspicious that underlying the legal jargon is some trick that will forever limit aboriginal rights and rob Canada's natives of what they say is rightfully theirs. Politicians counter that sections 25 and 35 offer Canada's natives the strongest possible protections. However, until these sections are tested in the Supreme Court, Canadians will have to live with two interpretations of them.

Despite the suspicion and uncertainty that now surround aboriginal rights, one group of natives has reason to celebrate. The Equality Rights provision in the Charter of Rights and Freedoms (subsection 15(1)) will finally make Indian women equal to Indian men. It seems certain that the nondiscrimination rule in this subsection will override the clause in the Indian Act (paragraph 12(1)(b)) that discriminates against Indian women.

The offending paragraph states that any Indian woman who marries a non-Indian loses her Indian status and cannot get it back. The same is not true for Indian men. In fact, if an Indian man marries a non-Indian woman then, under the Indian Act, that woman automatically becomes an Indian and is entitled to all benefits accompanying that status. Indian women have been fighting for years to have this situation changed and it appears that subsection 15(1) will finally do the job.

EQUALIZATION AND REGIONAL DISPARITIES

Part III of the Constitution Act 1982 contains only one section, 36, and is titled "Equalization and Regional Disparities." This unwieldly phrase can be translated into "revenue sharing between the rich and poor provinces." The principle of making equalization payments is well established in Canada. The idea is to ensure that the so-called "have not" provinces can enjoy a standard of living approximating that enjoyed by the "have" provinces. Since 1957 funds have been unconditionally transferred to the poorer provinces so that they could provide their residents with reasonable levels of public services without having to raise taxes to unrealistic levels.

Section 36 was accepted by all participants at the November 1981 first ministers conference on the Constitution. The prime minister and the premiers agreed that the diverse nature of a country as large as Canada makes wide gaps between the rich and the poor inevitable. To narrow that gap the objectives of equalizing opportunity and reducing economic disparity were placed in the Constitution and made the joint responsibility of the federal and provincial governments.

CONSTITUTIONAL CONFERENCE

Like Part III, Part IV consists of only one section; it is numbered 37 and titled "Constitutional Conference." The section

— commits the prime minister and the premiers to another constitutional conference,
— indicates that native rights will be a priority issue at that conference, and
— makes a commitment to include the territorial governments in discussions of interest to them.

Such a section is not of the sort most people expect to see in a constitution. In fact, it will not be in our Constitution for long. A later section, 54, states that section 37 will be in the Constitution only temporarily. One year after the Constitution comes into force section 37 will be automatically repealed. When that happens all sections following 36 will be renumbered sequentially, and section 54, its work completed, will also be dropped. But why were these temporary sections included at all?

Section 37 recognizes that though the November 1981 constitutional conference ended in substantial agreement, the first ministers did not complete everything they set out to accomplish. They did not come up with a satisfactory definition of aboriginal rights, they did not agree on a new division of powers between Ottawa and the provinces nor did they consider how to revise such institutions as the Senate and the Supreme Court. Section 37 is merely a guarantee that constitutional reform will not be set aside indefinitely, but will be formally considered at least one more time.

Section 37 does raise one unique problem. Can the constitutional requirement for "A constitutional conference composed of the Prime Minister of Canada and the first ministers of the provinces" be fulfilled if one premier refuses to attend? Quebec's René Lévesque was so incensed by the outcome of the November 1981 constitutional conference that he vowed never again to return to a first ministers constitutional conference. But section 37 seems to require Quebec's participation. This conflict raises both legal and ethical questions about how long Ottawa and the provinces can continue negotiations with one of the major partners in Confederation refusing to take part.

THE AMENDING FORMULA

The new Constitution contains not one amending formula but five. There are separate amending procedures for

1. Changes affecting only Parliament
2. Changes affecting only provincial legislatures
3. Changes affecting some but not all provinces
4. Changes to the monarchy, to basic institutions or to the status of Canada's official languages
5. All other constitutional amendments

Changes Affecting Parliament or Provincial Legislatures

Section 44. Subject to sections 41 and 42, Parliament may exclusively make laws amending the Constitution of Canada in relation to the executive government of Canada or the Senate and the House of Commons.

Section 45. Subject to section 41, the legislature of each province may exclusively make laws amending the constitution of the province.

These two amending procedures are very straightforward. They contain no power that was not already accorded the federal and provincial governments under the old Constitution. Very simply, both Parliament and the provincial legislatures retain the power to amend their own constitutions and to reform their own institutions, subject to certain exceptions specified in other sections. One exception, for example, is the office of the governor general. This is listed in section 41 as something that cannot be abolished or altered unless the federal and all the provincial governments so consent.

Changes Affecting Some But Not All Provinces

Section 43. An amendment to the Constitution of Canada in relation to any provision that applies to one or more, but not all, provinces, including
(a) any alteration to boundaries between provinces, and
(b) any amendment to any provision that relates to the use of the English or the French language within a province,
may be made by proclamation issued by the Governor General under the Great Seal of Canada only where so authorized

by resolutions of the Senate and House of Commons and of the legislative assembly of each province to which the amendment applies.

There was no legal way to amend the old Constitution of Canada if the reforms contemplated would have altered federal-provincial relations. That could only be done in and by Britain. This section removes Britain from the process, but it keeps alive a tradition that has developed since Confederation and that in most instances has been adhered to in Canada. That tradition is that no amendments affecting a province will be made without that province's consent.

By incorporating the existing tradition, this section streamlines amendments of limited scope by providing an exception to normal amending procedures, which require unanimous or near-unanimous consent for constitutional amendments. Under this section only Ottawa and those provinces directly affected need agree to constitutional amendments of less than national scope. If, for example, Quebec agreed to give up some of its territory to New Brunswick, only Quebec, New Brunswick, the Senate and the House of Commons would have to consent to the boundary change. This is far less cumbersome than the general amending formula (contained in section 38).

The Monarchy, Institutions and Official Languages

Section 41. An amendment to the Constitution of Canada in relation to the following matters may be made by proclamation issued by the Governor General under the Great Seal of Canada only where authorized by resolutions of the Senate and House of Commons and of the legislative assembly of each province:
(a) the office of the Queen, the Governor General and the Lieutenant Governor of a province;
(b) the right of a province to a number of members in the House of Commons not less than the number of Senators by which the province is entitled to be represented at the time this Part comes into force;
(c) subject to section 43, the use of the English or the French language;
(d) the composition of the Supreme Court of Canada; and
(e) an amendment to this Part.

A section similar to this one has been included in every amending formula ever seriously considered in Canada. What this section does is list five categories of amendments that deal with subjects so crucial to Canadian democracy that they may be made only with unanimous consent. The Senate, the House of Commons and the legislatures of each and every province all must agree to any change in the status of the items listed above.

All Other Constitutional Amendments: The General Amending Formula

Section 38. (1) An amendment to the Constitution of Canada may be made by proclamation issued by the Governor General under the Great Seal of Canada where so authorized by
(a) resolutions of the Senate and House of Commons; and
(b) resolutions of the legislative assemblies of at least two-thirds of the provinces that have, in the aggregate, according to the then latest general census, at least fifty per cent of the population of all the provinces.
(2) An amendment made under subsection (1) that derogates from the legislative powers, the proprietary rights or any other rights or privileges of the legislature or government of a province shall require a resolution supported by a majority of the members of each of the Senate, the House of Commons and the legislative assemblies required under subsection (1).

Subsection 38(1) outlines the general formula for amending the Constitution, the procedure that will be used most often. Each change requires

— A resolution passed by the Senate agreeing to the amendment in question
— A resolution passed by the House of Commons agreeing to the amendment
— A resolution of the legislatures of two-thirds of the provinces (seven out of ten) agreeing to the amendment. Those seven provinces must represent at least fifty percent of the population.

No province is given special status under this section, but it is clear that some will be "more equal," as the expression goes, than others. Ontario, Quebec and British Columbia are home to so many Canadians that the fifty percent population requirement will give them

more clout in future constitutional negotiations than such less popu-
lated provinces as Prince Edward Island and Newfoundland.

Subsection 38(2) adopts the "two-thirds, fifty percent" rule in the
previous subsection but it makes certain constitutional amendments
slightly more difficult to achieve. Any amendment designed to lessen
provincial power must be adopted by a majority of the members of
each voting body stipulated in 38(1). If all eleven governments are
majority governments, this will pose no problem. Conversely, if several
voting governments are minority governments, constitutional reform
may be made an even more cumbersome and difficult proposition than
it will be normally.

> Section 38. (3) An amendment referred to in subsection (2) shall
> not have effect in a province the legislative assembly of which
> has expressed its dissent thereto by resolution supported by a
> majority of its members prior to the issue of the proclamation
> to which the amendment relates unless that legislative assem-
> bly, subsequently, by resolution supported by a majority of its
> members, revokes its dissent and authorizes the amendment.
> (4) A resolution of dissent made for the purposes of subsec-
> tion (3) may be revoked at any time before or after the issue of
> the proclamation to which it relates.

This is the so-called "opting-out" provision. Under the general amending formula, once Ottawa and seven provinces with fifty percent of the
population agree to a constitutional change, the whole country is
bound by that agreement. Even the dissenting provinces are bound. If,
however, the change reduces provincial rights or powers, subsection
38(3) allows as many as three provinces to refuse to go along with the
majority. If they refuse they will not be bound by the amendment
provision.

Subsection 38(4) simply allows a dissenting province to change its
mind and revoke its previous resolution of disassociation—in colloquial
terms, to "opt back in." There is no time limit after which a province
cannot change its mind. A dissenting province can opt back into the
provisions of a constitutional amendment at any time. However, no
province can opt out after it has given assent and the law has been
proclaimed.

With all of the resolutions necessary to complete the general
amending procedure, a considerable amount of time could elapse
between the time when a constitutional conference agreed to an
amendment and the day that amendment was proclaimed and took

effect. In an effort to hurry that process along somewhat without imposing impossible deadlines, section 39 gives every province at least one year to make up its mind about supporting or rejecting a proposed amendment and ensures that no proposed amendment will remain outstanding for more than three years. If after three years a proposed amendment has not been duly adopted by the resolutions of the Senate, House of Commons and seven provincial legislatures, then it automatically expires. In order to reactivate it the amending procedure would have to be started all over again.

A later subsection, 46(2), allows any province that assents to or opts into a proposed amendment to opt out or cancel its assent at any time before the amendment is proclaimed law. Future attempts to make constitutional changes in Canada could result in some rather dramatic seasaw battles. Those provinces favouring an amendment and those opposing it could, in turn, pressure indifferent provinces, conceivably causing them to opt back and forth, in and out, of an amendment a number of times before the three-year limitation period expired. In the case of particularly controversial amendments, the question of whether or not sufficient provincial agreement exists may remain uncertain until the last moment.

> Section 40. Where an amendment is made under subsection 38(1) that transfers provincial legislative powers relating to education or other cultural matters from provincial legislatures to Parliament, Canada shall provide reasonable compensation to any province to which the amendment does not apply.

This section requires Ottawa to compensate financially any province that opts out of any amendment that shifts educational or cultural jurisdiction to the federal government. If, for example, every province except Nova Scotia were to give Ottawa control over secondary education, the federal government would have to help Nova Scotia shoulder the burden of retaining its own separate education system.

This section represents a victory for the federal government's point of view that opting out should be discouraged. The fear is that every time one or more provinces opt out of a constitutional change it becomes more difficult to describe the Canadian Constitution. The federal government opposed the whole notion of opting out in its effort to ensure that the Constitution as the fundamental law of the land would be uniformly applied across Canada. The provinces wanted section 40 to provide monetary compensation in the case of all opting out. Supporters of the federal position hope that the compromise that limits compensation for opting out to the areas of education and culture will ultimately make decisions to opt out financially unwise and therefore, infrequent. If, for example, the provinces agreed to hand jurisdiction over highways to Ottawa, a province would have to think long and hard about opting out of that amendment because its taxpayers would be left with the cost of all future road construction and repair.

Section 42. (1) An amendment to the Constitution of Canada in relation to the following matters may be made only in accordance with subsection 38(1):
(a) the principle of proportionate representation of the provinces in the House of Commons prescribed by the Constitution of Canada;
(b) the powers of the Senate and the method of selecting Senators;
(c) the number of members by which a province is entitled to be represented in the Senate and the residence qualifications of Senators;
(d) subject to paragraph 41(d), the Supreme Court of Canada;
(e) the extension of existing provinces into the territories; and
(f) notwithstanding any other law or practice, the establishment of new provinces.
(2) Subsections 38(2) to (4) do not apply in respect of amendments in relation to matters referred to in subsection (1).

Subsection 42(1) merely lists a number of areas that can only be amended using the general amending provisions in subsection 38(1). The list is not exhaustive. It is simply intended to dispel any doubts about the fundamental aspects of the Canadian democratic system set out in paragraphs (a) to (f). Even if arguments could be made that one or more of the items listed could theoretically be amended under one of the simpler procedures, this subsection dictates that the general provisions must be employed. If, for example, only Manitoba wished to extend its boundaries northward into the Northwest Territories and attempted to do so under the simple amending provisions of section 43, it could not. Paragraph (e) of subsection 42(1) states that such a boundary change must be authorized by the Senate, House of Commons and seven provinces.

Subsection 42(2) attempts to place the importance of the items listed in 42(1) into perspective. They are not so important that a majority resolution rather than a simple resolution is needed to approve them (see 38(2)) but they are important enough that no province can opt out of any amendment to them (see 38(3) and (4)).

Finally, in order to understand completely the new amending procedure the roles of the governor general and of the Senate should be examined. The phrase "made by proclamation issued by the Governor General under the Great Seal of Canada" occurs over and over again in the various sections of the amending procedures. In Canada no law can take effect until it is proclaimed, signed and sealed by the governor general. It is a ceremonial function only, for though the governor general technically has the power to do so, no governor general (except perhaps under unimaginably extraordinary circumstances) would refuse to sign and seal a bill or resolution that had been properly passed by Parliament. Still, the Constitution pays traditional respect to the fact that until proclaimed, no constitutional amendment can take effect.

Like the governor general, the Senate appears to have powers under the amending formula equal to those of the House of Commons and the provincial legislatures. All major amendments require Senate approval. However, in practical terms, that approval can be dispensed with. Section 47 abolishes the Senate's absolute veto power over constitutional amendments and replaces it with what is known as a "suspensive veto." If the Senate opposes a proposed amendment, it can refuse to pass the required consenting resolution. That leaves the House of Commons with two options: It can accede to the Senate's opinion and let the matter die or it can wait 180 days and then repass the resolution. The second adoption of an amendment resolution by the House of Commons bypasses the Upper House and dispenses with the normal requirement for the latter's consent.

There are many who argue that, appearances aside, section 47 actually strengthens the Senate's power over constitutional reform. The Upper House already has the absolute right to veto normal federal legislation but, in fact, never uses it. There seems to be a feeling among senators that, despite their theoretical power, it would somehow be inappropriate for an appointed body to overrule the country's democratically elected lawmakers. The same feeling may vanish under the suspensive rule in section 47. Now that the Senate's opinion is not final on constitutional amendments, it may be more likely to give it.

Tomorrow's Constitution

The pursuit of constitutional reform in Canada is far from finished. From the provincial point of view, especially, the battle has only just begun. In large part, the November 1981 agreement between Ottawa and nine of the provinces—the historic agreement that gave birth to the new Constitution—was made possible only because the premiers at that meeting set aside most of their constitutional demands. Agreement was reached on patriation, a charter of rights and an amending formula, but for many of Canada's premiers, these are not critical issues.

The premiers are chiefly interested in two many-faceted issues: (1) a new division of power in Canada and (2) a stronger provincial presence in federal institutions. The first ministers last dealt with these issues at the September 1980 constitutional conference. That conference, by the admission of all participants, ended in total failure. In February 1979 and October 1978 the first ministers also concentrated on power sharing and institutional reform. Those conferences, too, ended in failure. To be fair, the 1979 conference saw Ottawa and the provinces come close to agreement on a number of issues, and a "best efforts" list of proposals was even published. In the final analysis, however, those near-agreements produced no actual constitutional reforms.

What seems to be the undoing of every federal-provincial constitutional conference is a deep-rooted disagreement on what Canadian

73

federalism means. The provinces see Canada as a group of communities, a collection of ten near-sovereign states, each of which is better able to govern its own resident Canadians than is the federal government in Ottawa. Provincial politicians maintain that they, being closest to the people, are the most keenly aware of the special needs and aspirations of their regions of Canada.

Working from this vantage point, the provinces contend that the federal government would best serve Canadian interests by limiting its sphere of influence to administering the few areas of government that by their very nature require a single overview rather than ten separate approaches. For example, provincial representatives consider uniformity across Canada desirable in the areas of national defence, international treaty enforcement and criminal legislation. Conversely, the same provincial representatives think economic policy, industrial strategies, the development, taxation and sale of natural resources, social security, health care, education, communications and many other important areas of jurisdiction are best left to the individual provincial governments.

Federal representatives counter with the view that uncertainty and regional disparity would inevitably flow from decentralization on the scale suggested by many provinces. They point, as well, to the European Economic Community as an example of how other countries have agreed to set aside some of their nationalistic self-interests so that they can band together and thereby emulate the sort of federal system already enjoyed in Canada.

Negotiating constitutional reform from this basic philosophical position, the federal government has pressed for *tighter* central control over the economy and over other crucial areas such as communications, social security and even education. As a trade-off Ottawa has suggested that various institutions of the federal government be restructured so as to give the provinces more input into federal decision making. The federal theory is simply this: Decentralization is out of the question because it will weaken the country. The only alternative, then, is to satisfy provincial demands for more power by changing institutions, such as the Senate and perhaps even the House of Commons, so as to make them better reflect regional interests.

So far the provinces have not rejected the federal alternative, but neither have they set aside their own aspirations. In fact, a number of premiers have suggested that the provincial and federal concepts of federalism be acted upon simultaneously. This would have the effect of shifting most power to the provinces while at the same time giving them greater control in Ottawa. Needless to say, this suggestion has found very few supporters among federal representatives.

The first ministers are constitutionally committed to holding another conference before 17 April 1983. Division of powers and reform of federal institutions will be the major topics of discussion. The subjects within these two broad areas can be broken into three categories:

1. *Areas where the federal government wants more power.* The major issue here is who shall control the economy. The federal government maintains that the provinces have abused their economic powers and thereby weakened Canada's effectiveness as an economic union. Ottawa believes that it has allowed too much control over the economy to slip into provincial hands and it wants some back.
2. *Areas where the provinces want expanded powers at the expense of the federal government.* Quite often concerns are regionalized: Coastal provinces want to discuss jurisdiction over fishing; Alberta is interested in reopening talks on the taxing of natural resources. There are, in fact, dozens of areas over which the provinces want more control, but in the immediate future talks are likely to be concentrated on communications, offshore resources, fisheries and family law.
3. *Areas where both Ottawa and the provinces have stated a preference for change.* The emphasis here is likely to be on how best to reform two federal institutions—the Senate and the Supreme Court of Canada. The common goal has always been to give the provinces more say in the make-up and workings of these two elements of federal government. As has been noted, however, the two levels of government differ on whether institutional reform should complement a redivision of power or be substituted for it.

The following is a breakdown of where the federal and provincial governments appear to stand on the key issues. It is not intended to be the final word on any subject nor does it presume to reflect every detail of either side's thinking. The purpose is to outline some of the various proposals that have been made in order to give the reader a starting point from which to follow future negotiations.

THE STRUGGLE FOR CONTROL OVER THE ECONOMY

The key issue in the struggle for economic control is whether or not some description of Canada as an economic union should be enshrined in the Constitution. This issue goes to the very heart of the disagreement between Ottawa and the provinces about the nature of Canadian federalism. Ottawa insists that discriminatory provincial hiring and trade practices create economic barriers that limit freedom of choice and that will eventually result in the economic balkanization of the country. Provincial governments recognize the value of totally free trade and commerce among the provinces but still wish to be able to pass laws favouring their own residents and industries.

Ottawa is concerned that over the past two decades or so the federal government has allowed the provinces to develop too much economic clout. By law Ottawa has just about all the economic power in Canada. The Constitution gives it wide taxing and borrowing power, as well as power over interest rates, currency, coinage and banking. In practice, however, Ottawa has allowed much of the economic influence in Canada to pass into the hands of the premiers. The federal government may collect the majority of the tax dollars in the country, but it allows the provinces to spend most of them. Enormous amounts of federally collected revenues are distributed to the provinces to finance major programs such as education and health care.

The provincial role in economic policy and planning has grown enormously. First ministers conferences on the economy have now become accepted precursors to massive shifts in economic policy. Premiers complain bitterly when the federal government changes economic direction without prior consultation with the provinces. The result is that a new concept of economic responsibility has grown up in Canada. The Constitution may give most economic powers to the federal government, but practice and public perceptions make for a quite different economic reality.

Even if the federal government decided to roll back the political clock, to ignore the realities of federal-provincial relations, and to apply strictly the provisions of the BNA Act, it could not necessarily establish the sort of economic union it wants. The BNA Act would enable Ottawa to reclaim all or most of the economic clout it has lost, but it would not enable Ottawa to force the provinces to set aside their isolationist policies.

The BNA Act's prohibition against provincial isolationism is very limited and its guarantee of an unimpeded economic union very general. Section 121 of the Act prohibits only such flagrant examples of provincial protectionism as tariff barriers between provinces. Section 121 reads

> Section 121. All Articles of the Growth, Produce, or Manufacture of any one of the Provinces shall, from and after the Union, be admitted free into each of the other Provinces.

The constitutional guarantees that the federal government is seeking are far broader than those in section 121.

Ottawa has proposed a replacement clause for section 121, a far-reaching guarantee of economic union that would accomplish the following:

1. Contain a general rule guaranteeing absolutely free and nondiscriminatory trade and commerce practices
2. Give Parliament two legal reasons for derogating from the general rule:
   (a) to further the principles of equalization, and
   (b) to act in situations of near national emergency
3. Give two reasons, as well, for provincial derogation:
   (a) to establish residency tests for social services, and
   (b) to promote equalization within a province
4. Maintain the prohibition against tariffs in the present section 121
5. Provide for enforcement by the courts with appeals either to higher courts or to a new Upper House

Whether Canadians will ever see an economic union so clearly enshrined in the Constitution is difficult to say. Many of the premiers strongly suspect that such guarantees would rob them of the power to control vital elements of their own economies, while giving them nothing in return. Nevertheless, the federal government is unlikely to give up the struggle for a stronger economic union than that described in the BNA Act.

Mobility Rights, section 6 of the Charter of Rights and Freedoms, is an example of the sort of compromise Ottawa and the provinces can make. In exchange for guaranteeing all Canadians the right to live and work in any province, the federal government agreed to include a clause giving the provinces certain affirmative action powers. Any province with higher than average unemployment may legally institute hiring practices that favour local residents. Residency tests are established by the provinces.

The new mobility rights, however, do not go far enough for the federal government. These rights apply only to people. Ottawa also wants to guarantee the free flow of goods, services and capital among the provinces. Most provincial leaders are willing to consider such guarantees, but only if the Constitution contains clauses allowing the provinces to get around the free-flow rule in certain circumstances. In the same way as the new mobility rights allow for affirmative action in high unemployment areas, the provinces contend that any further guarantees of economic union should also allow exceptions.

No agreement has been reached on what exceptions might be included, although a number of possible exception rules or formulas have been proposed. Some premiers want special rules that would allow ''have not'' provinces to discriminate in favour of local industries. Other premiers maintain that at the very least enterprises owned by a province should be made automatic exceptions and should be allowed to enjoy legislated trade advantages or favourable provincial buying policies. The difficulty extends beyond the need for agreement on a set of exception rules: Enforcement is also a source of contention. Who will be the final arbiter of a dispute between Ottawa and the provinces over the application of the exception rules?

The federal government prefers pure judicial enforcement. It believes that once an economic union is in place, any laws that appear to violate it should be laid before a court. The court would then be charged with deciding whether or not the law in question came within the terms of whatever exception rule had been adopted. If the law failed to meet the requirements, the court would be empowered to strike it down.

Provincial governments recommend other review procedures. Many of them wish to see a restructured Senate, with members appointed by the provinces, charged with the job. At the very least many premiers believe some combination of court and Upper House should rule. The combination approach would work like this: A province would pass legislation that it believed came within the exception rules to the economic union. Any challenge would be launched in the courts. The losing side would have the right to appeal the court's decision to the new Upper House. Still other provincial representatives have suggested that first ministers conferences could be convened to deal with possible infractions.

What seems likely is that in the months preceding future constitutional conferences the federal government will try to marshal public opinion behind the concept of a stronger economic union. Attacks on provincial protectionism will probably grow as Ottawa attempts to paint economic regionalism as destructive. The value of the big and competitive market for products that only a Canada-wide economic policy can provide will be stressed in public addresses by cabinet ministers and perhaps even in the sort of advocacy advertising on television that was the hallmark of the federal information drive during the 1980-81 constitutional negotiations. Centralization will be depicted as efficient and competitive, decentralization as the certain route to economic ruin.

The counterattack by the provinces will stress the values of regional sensitivity and the dangers of certain Canada-wide policies. For example, Saskatchewan contends that it needs discriminatory laws to protect its farm-based economy and points with pride to a present law that forbids out-of-province land speculators from buying Saskatchewan farms and driving the cost of land up and beyond the means of resident farmers. Industrialized provinces such as Quebec complain of federal insensitivity to failing industries in the textile and footwear sectors. The success or failure of Ottawa's continuing drive for a stronger economic union may depend on which side of the debate wins the support of the Canadian people.

PROVINCIAL DEMANDS FOR EXPANDED POWERS

Communications

The basic approaches of the two levels of government to the communications issue mirror their approaches to constitutional reform generally. From the federal point of view, the national and international characteristics of modern communications outweigh any local or regional concerns. Ottawa believes that broadcasting must be seen and therefore regulated as one single Canadian system. In the federal government's opinion, only a centrally controlled regulatory body is suitable for such a task.

Provincial governments tend to look more at communications output than at delivery systems, that is more at *products* such as television and radio broadcasts than at the microwave or satellite systems that deliver those products. The products, argue the provinces, have a tremendous impact on local cultural and economic goals and, therefore, should be regulated by a government that is in tune with local needs—a provincial government. All ten provinces agree that there are national and international aspects to communications, but they favour a shared jurisdiction in these areas. In most instances, however, they want that shared jurisdiction constructed so as to give the provinces the final decision-making power in cases of deadlock.

There are four main areas of communications upon which federal-provincial negotiations concentrate:

1. *Radio Frequency Spectrum.* The issue here is who controls the airwaves? At stake is control over AM, FM and shortwave broadcasting. This is presently a federal area of responsibility, but the provinces would like to share jurisdiction in the future.
2. *Broadcasting.* This heading covers everything from national television networks, such as CTV, to local stations. At present, all aspects of broadcasting are under federal control. The provinces would like to take over the local aspects of the broadcasting field.
3. *Cable Television.* Ideally the provinces would like total control over cable, which is now an exclusively federal concern. The most likely solution is a system of shared jurisdiction: Ottawa would control cable services that extend beyond any one province's boundaries and the provinces would be given control over local undertakings such as closed-circuit networks.
4. *Telecommunications Carriers and Rates.* This is a complex area that deals with many things—from satellites to the cost of a phone call. Ottawa has suggested splitting jurisdiction: Local networks would go to the provinces and national or international undertakings (such as CNCP, TELESAT and TELEGLOBE) would stay in federal hands. The provinces want not only shared control over everything but also the final decision-making power in a deadlock.

Clearly, at least one side will have to move a long way on the communications issue or it will not be solved in the near future. The federal government may be forced to move first. Closed-circuit cable networks are now being created in Canada. These are networks that do not rely on satellite or airwave transmissions. They utilize no antennas but are pure cable networks that broadcast only prerecorded programs contained on video cassettes. The courts may declare that such networks belong under provincial control, reasoning that they are not part of a larger national network of cables, ground stations, airwaves, microwaves or satellites, but rather, purely local undertakings. If that happens the federal monopoly over broadcasting will be broken. Its monopoly gone, Ottawa might be more amenable to sharing jurisdiction in some areas. It is unlikely, however, that such shared jurisdiction would ever be constructed in such a way as to give the provinces the sort of ultimate decision-making power they are seeking.

Offshore Resources

Ottawa and the provinces are so far apart in their basic approaches to offshore resources that final settlement of this issue is unlikely to be reached quickly. Essentially, the provincial view is that coastal provinces should enjoy the same rights, privileges and responsibilities pertaining to offshore resources as other provinces now enjoy for onshore resources. The federal government feels that such a transfer of power to coastal provinces would not be in the best interests of all Canadians. Its view is that an administrative arrangement that allows for joint management and federal ownership should be worked out. The rationale behind this approach is that joint management would bring great new wealth to coastal provinces but still enable Ottawa to direct the production of offshore resources so as to benefit all of the country.

One of the major problems confronting both levels of government is the question of exactly where ownership of offshore resources now lies. In 1967 the Supreme Court ruled that the resources off British Columbia's coast belong to the federal government. With the exception of Newfoundland, the other coastal provinces are probably bound by that ruling; resources off their shores are owned and controlled by the federal government.

Newfoundland's situation may be unique because of the special terms under which it agreed to join Confederation in 1949. One of those terms appears to give Newfoundland special rights offshore, but until the Supreme Court clarifies what those special rights are no one can say whether or not they include outright resource ownership. Moreover, even if the Court does decide that Newfoundland has special power over offshore resources, the Court could still interpret that power in such a way as to include only those resources found within three, twelve or some other narrow band of miles around the island. Such a ruling would cut the province off from the great oil wealth in the Hibernia fields, which lie approximately 190 miles off shore.

Even if the federal government agreed to transfer jurisdiction to the provinces, defining ownership would be a complex problem. The real difficulty would be in determining who gets what: Eight provinces and two territories have valid claims to offshore resources. A quick glance at the map of Canada is sufficient to demonstrate the difficulty of delineating claims to what could amount to millions of square miles of untapped wealth. Where does one draw the boundary line between Nova Scotia and Prince Edward Island, between Manitoba and Ontario (through Hudson Bay), between Labrador and Quebec or between New Brunswick and the four other provinces that border on the Gulf of St. Lawrence?

Finally, if domestic claims were settled, the problem would still be only half solved. A challenging list of international disputes would remain; currently there are jurisdictional disputes with the mainland United States, Alaska, Greenland, the USSR and France through its island colonies, St. Pierre and Miquelon. All of these have valid and conflicting claims to ocean riches. Moreover, they do not want to negotiate separate treaties with each individual province. As sovereign nations, these other countries want to deal with Canada as a whole, with the federal government. So, even if Ottawa wanted to give up jurisdiction completely, it would be under considerable international pressure not to do so.

Provincial representatives are confident that boundary problems, both national and international, can be overcome, that Ottawa's role as Canada's international representative is not necessarily incompatible with provincial ownership and that "Canada first" agreements can be devised to ensure that resources such as offshore gas and oil are made available to Canadians on a priority basis. Their confidence has failed to impress the federal government or to move it from its preference for a joint-management approach to offshore resource development.

The federal government has made a four-point proposal for joint management. Federal government representatives say their proposal would leave legal ownership of offshore resources in federal hands but would ensure maximum benefits to coastal provinces. The federal plan would work like this:

1. *Revenue Sharing.* As long as a coastal province remained a "have not" province, it would receive all revenues from royalties, fees, rentals and payments for exploration and development rights. Once the province became a "have" province, its share of these revenues would decrease until, ultimately, it was receiving revenues similar to those now enjoyed by the governments of Alberta, British Columbia and Saskatchewan for their land-based resources.

2. *Management.* Overall management of all aspects of offshore development would be undertaken by a joint-management board consisting of three federal and three provincial members and a neutral chairperson. This management team would at-

tempt to give priority consideration to provincial concerns except where they directly conflicted with the national interest.

3. *Legislation.* The governing legislation would be those laws containing the federal government's national energy policy.

4. *Constitutional Confirmation.* The federal government has not been specific about how this would be achieved but has undertaken to develop appropriate wording to include its joint-management concept in the Constitution.

Clearly, a compromise between joint management and outright provincial ownership and control will have to be reached if the issue of offshore resources is to be settled permanently. The federal proposal has some room for movement. The provincial share of revenues could be increased or provincial taxing powers over resources expanded. In particular, the key questions of rate of development and environmental controls could be placed more clearly within the provincial sphere of interest.

What is far from clear is the degree of urgency that surrounds this issue. Ottawa has negotiated a number of energy agreements—with Alberta, Saskatchewan, British Columbia and Nova Scotia. As long as new agreements can be reached and old ones renegotiated, it may be that the spirit of cooperation will relieve the pressure for final constitutional solutions. Without pressure for compromise, Canadians may have to wait a long time for a constitutional settlement of the offshore resources issue to grow out of today's starkly conflicting views.

Fisheries

There is no question about who controls Canadian fisheries today. The British North America Act gives control over all sea coast and inland fishing to the federal government. Few provincial representatives are satisfied with this situation. With the exception of Nova Scotia, which welcomes a continued federal presence in certain specified areas, the provinces are demanding that almost total jurisdiction over fisheries be transferred to them.

There are four major areas of jurisdiction at stake:

1. Marine fisheries
2. Inland fisheries
3. Fish farming of immobile species, such as oysters, and
4. Anadromous species of fish, such as salmon, which leave the ocean and swim inland to spawn

The federal government has agreed to give to the provinces total control over fish farming and, subject to two conditions, control over inland fishing. However, Ottawa has rejected provincial demands for full or, at the very least, shared control over the other two areas: marine and anadromous. Nova Scotia supports the federal notion of continued federal control over marine and anadromous fish combined with a constitutional commitment by Ottawa to consult with the provinces before making major policy changes in the field of marine fisheries.

The two conditions that Ottawa has placed on the transfer of inland fisheries to the provinces deal with fish habitat and Indian food fishery rights. Ottawa wants to maintain responsibility for the fish habitat by continuing to regulate activities that affect salmon streams and waterways that are not totally contained inside a single province's boundaries. The point here is to guarantee that mining, lumbering and other activities do not threaten the environment or spawning grounds of fish. The federal government also contends that the provinces should guarantee to honour traditional Indian fishing rights before any control over inland fishing is transferred into provincial hands. So far, the provinces have not agreed to these impediments to absolute control. Their reasons are not clear, though it is believed that provincial representatives think the provinces can protect the fish habitat as well as Ottawa and that Indians should not be accorded priority status or any right to override provincial laws.

Future constitutional conferences will probably explore the possibility of either splitting the various issues or of devising a system of concurrent controls. Like so many other outstanding issues, the secret to resolving this one may lie in creation of a new Upper House. If that problem could ever be worked out so as to give the provinces real input into policy making at the federal level, the sense of mistrust that clouds negotiations of shared control might evaporate.

Family Law

Of all the issues that have been discussed at constitutional conferences where a redivision of power between Ottawa and the provinces was on the agenda, none has come closer to resolution than family law. Under the present Constitution jurisdiction over family law is divided between the two levels of government. The federal government makes laws dealing with marriage and divorce; the provincial governments make laws dealing with the division of property when marriage ends in separation, with some custody matters and maintenance orders and with the solemnization of marriage. For years Ottawa and the provinces have been trying to hammer out a unified approach to family law.

The most widely favoured approach gives nearly total control over all aspects of family law to the provinces. Provincial governments would establish the grounds and the rules governing eligibility for a divorce. Provincial courts would be charged with disposing of all family law problems from divorce to custody to maintenance orders. The federal government's role would be extremely limited. Its sole responsibility would be to devise a set of guidelines by which the validity of divorces from different jurisdictions could be tested. For example, no Canadian could go to Mexico for a "quickie" divorce unless Mexican divorces met the basic requirements established by Ottawa.

While the provinces are eager to assume jurisdiction over family law, their enthusiasm is not shared by many of the lawyers, counsellors and court officials who work in the field. Many of these people believe that handing more power to the provinces is exactly the opposite of what should be happening. They would like to see a uniform national system of family law. Further decentralization of the system, they say, will only lead to abuses. Their fear is that fragmentation of family law jurisdiction will lead to uncertainty and frustration for those seeking relief from the courts.

The possibility of different divorce rules in different provinces, say the critics, may result in "forum shopping," that is, in some sort of Reno situation where people try to obtain divorces in "easier" provinces. The critics maintain that no guidelines set forth by the federal government could prevent this situation from developing to some extent. The enforcement of custody orders, alimony payments and child-support payments could become even more difficult than it now is unless each province is bound by the judicial orders of all the rest. The problem of "kidnapping" by parents who lose custody battles could escalate.

The provincial response to these fears is that all of them can be overcome by careful legal drafting. A constitutional provision that required every province to recognize the family law orders of the others could be enacted. Residency rules could be adopted to stop people from moving into a province simply to take advantage of its divorce laws. The overall philosophy of provincial representatives is that the family law system is currently too disjointed and that they will do whatever is necessary to guarantee uniformity. They will most probably get the chance—unless there is an abrupt change in thinking, it now appears likely that family law jurisdiction will be transferred to the provinces during the next round of constitutional negotiations.

THE REFORM OF FEDERAL INSTITUTIONS

The Upper House

Everyone, it seems, wants to reform the Senate. Suggestions have come from all directions: from the Liberal government, the Conservative opposition in Parliament, the Pepin-Robarts Commission, the Canadian Bar Association, provincial governments and political parties and a variety of special interests groups. Each recommendation has outlined new powers, membership requirements, appointment or election procedures, internal rules and voting procedures. No suggestion has yet received unanimous federal-provincial support.

No government recommendation—federal or provincial—has called for an elected Upper House; all have favoured membership by appointment. Just who should make the appointments, however, is far from settled. In its 1978 constitutional proposal (Bill C-60) the federal government recommended a Senate of 118 members to be called the House of the Federation. Half of the members were to be selected by the provinces and half by the federal government. During the summer of 1980 federal and provincial cabinet ministers responsible for constitutional negotiations attempted to hammer out a common front on Senate reform. The earlier House of the Federation idea was not acceptable to provincial ministers but they could not agree upon a clear alternative.

The best the federal and provincial ministers could manage during that summer of negotiation was to recommend an interim solution. The Senate would remain, but a third federal chamber would be created and called the Council of the Provinces. This council would have thirty members, three from each province, appointed by provincial governments. Each provincial group of three would be required to vote as a block. The council's power would be limited to ratifying certain specified federal actions that directly affected provincial powers.

This interim suggestion for the creation of yet another federal institution was not adopted by the prime minister and the premiers at the September 1980 constitutional conference (the last first ministers conference to deal with Senate reform). However, neither was it rejected outright. It is probably safe to assume, though, that it will never be acted upon. In 1980 there was considerable pressure on Ottawa and the provinces to stop the constitutional bickering, work out some agreement and bring the Constitution home. With the new Constitution in place that pressure has vanished. Interim solutions are no longer needed to demonstrate federal-provincial cooperation, and everyone agrees they are really no solution at all. Now any reform of the Upper House will have to be final.

The Supreme Court

The old Constitution made no mention of the Supreme Court of Canada; nor does the new one. The BNA Act merely gave Parliament the power to establish "a General Court of Appeal for Canada" (section 101). The Supreme Court was founded on 8 April 1875, less than eight years after Confederation. It then consisted of a chief justice and five other justices. Not until 1949 was the Court expanded to nine justices. Each justice is a federal appointee and sits on the bench until the age of seventy-five. Generally speaking, the political attitude toward the Supreme Court is identical to that toward the Senate. There is much talk about changing it but no consensus about how that should be done.

There is general agreement on what aspects of the Court need altering. Most recommendations call for the following:

— More provincial input into appointments
— Constitutionally fixed quotas governing where appointments must come from
— Alternating chief justices between Quebec and non-Quebec appointments
— Giving the provinces the same right Ottawa now has of referring legal problems directly to the Court

The question of how to break these broad areas down to a final detailed agreement, however, is far from answered. Nearly every province has put forward a separate proposal for change though, oddly enough, most premiers take the position that they really have very few complaints with the Court as it now stands.

Which, if any, of the many variations available might ultimately gain universal acceptance is a wide-open question. The federal government is taking the position that the provinces, if they want a reformed High Court, should decide what the reforms will be. In 1978 Ottawa proposed an eleven-member bench (four from Quebec, seven from the rest of Canada), but the current federal attitude is that it will go along with anything the provinces agree to.

The two obvious questions are how long will the federal government maintain its compliant stand and how long will it take the provinces to agree? Any answer to the former question would be pure speculation but there is some evidence that the answer to the latter may be a long long time. The real stumbling block is the size and make-up of any restructured Court. All provincial representatives want constitutional guarantees of provincial involvement in future appointments and an appointment procedure that insists upon all regions of Canada being represented on the bench, but most appear to favour an expanded Court only to please Quebec.

Except in criminal law matters, Quebec's legal system is different from the rest of the country. Instead of following the English tradition of common law, Quebec uses a legal system that has its roots in Napoleon's France, the Civil Code. Because its law is so different, Quebec takes the position that there should be more Quebec lawyers or civilians on the bench than there are now. To this end it has called for either an expanded court or a system of dividing up the Court so that matters touching Quebec will be heard by a panel containing a majority of Quebec appointments. However, now that René Lévesque has vowed never again to attend another constitutional conference, no one can say whether or not the other premiers will continue to push for a larger Court merely to appease Quebec.

Perhaps the final word on changing the Supreme Court should go to the justices themselves. After all, they will have to work within the confines of whatever structure is finally adopted. The present justices like the present system. They do not favour the American style of appointments, which they feel politicizes the bench, nor do they feel it is wise to make the ratio between Quebec and non-Quebec judges such an issue. Such action, they feel, only lends credence to the misapprehension that judicial decisions are somehow affected by where a judge was born. On the subject of numbers, the Court's opinion is perhaps best summed up by one of its members, Mr. Justice Willard Estey, who likened an eleven-justice Court to an eighty-seven-man choir. The consensus on the bench seems to be that nine justices is about the maximum number manageable.

Afterword

The next decades will see the emergence of a new Canada. The changes that will flow from today's Constitution will be wide-sweeping; the changes that tomorrow's Constitution will bring could well be revolutionary. As the twentieth century draws to a close, three distinct voices are entering into an historic dialogue that will define Canada at the dawn of the twenty-first century—the voices of the judiciary, of governments and of the Canadian people.

THE NEW JUDICIARY

The role of the courts in shaping Canadian life is about to change dramatically. Nowhere will the change be more sharply felt than in the Supreme Court. In the past, Supreme Court justices have not been subjected to public scrutiny before their appointments, nor have their opinions had so significant an impact on government policy as to be examined under the same harsh light as are those of politicians. The new Constitution shifts that harsh light on the justices. The Charter of Rights and Freedoms will flood the courts with requests for interpretations of just what the first ministers meant when they enshrined this right or that in the Constitution. When these requests are granted hearing in the Supreme Court, the interpretations rendered by the justices will carry the full weight of constitutional law. The opinions of the Court will be reversible only by the lengthy and complex process of constitutional amendment.

Both levels of government are now scrutinizing their statute books in an effort to weed out offending laws before they are challenged. Censorship laws, labour laws, hiring practices, taxation laws applicable to one sex but not the other, language laws, landlord and tenant laws, immigration laws and procedures, all of these and dozens of others may run afoul of the new Charter. If they do, they must be redesigned to come within the exception rules in the Constitution or else the courts will strike them down.

Striking down laws will not be a novel experience for the High Court. Over the years, the judges have been asked to declare many federal and provincial laws invalid and in a number of instances they have complied. Up until now, however, all "invalid" or "unconstitutional" meant was that the law in question had been passed by the wrong level of government. Either Ottawa had tried to legislate in an area of exclusive provincial jurisdiction or vice versa. Now, if a law violates the Charter the Court will declare not that the wrong level of government has passed the law, but that no level of government can pass such a law. Power in Canada must now be exercised subject to three conditions: Some laws can only be passed by Parliament, others by a provincial legislature, but a third class of laws, those that violate the Charter, may be enacted by *no one*. The Supreme Court is now the ultimate arbiter of the exercise of power in Canada.

THE FUTURE OF CONSTITUTIONAL REFORM

The task ahead is nothing short of the creation of a new democracy in Canada. The issues that remain on the table of constitutional reform are the very issues that will define the Canada of tomorrow—indeed, they touch on every aspect of Canadian government and life. Yet Canadians who watched the creation of the Charter of Rights and Freedoms, the amending formula and the other provisions of the Constitution Act 1982 know how bitterly the representatives of federal and provincial governments—the prime negotiators—fought over these issues.

Unfortunately, the agreement on the new Constitution has not healed the wounds caused by the federal-provincial negotiations that produced that agreement. Quebec is in isolation. There is a feeling in some other provincial camps that somehow the federal government got what it wanted, the provinces got almost nothing. There is a feeling in Ottawa that the provinces can never be satisfied so why go on trying. The spirit of cooperative federalism is hardly alive and well in Canada.

At a news conference in Ottawa on 25 February 1982, Prime Minister Trudeau was asked whether or not he had privately told the premiers that cooperative federalism was dead. This is part of the exchange between the reporter and Mr. Trudeau:

Prime Minister Trudeau: I don't recall that I said "co-operative federalism" because what is it? I don't know. But the old type of federalism where we give money to the provinces, where they kick us in the teeth because they didn't get enough and they go around and spend it and say, of course, it is all from us, that type of federalism is finished . . .

Reporter: You think that is going to make the government more popular in the long run do you?

Prime Minister Trudeau: I don't know. The aim of government is not to be popular; the aim of a political party is to be popular. The aim of government, I think, is to govern, and I think we have tried governing through consensus; we have tried governing by being generous to the provinces, you will recall, even in the constitutional area; and we have tried governing in 1979 by offering a rather massive transfer of power to the provinces, and that was never enough. So we have changed that and we have said on the Constitution as we are doing on the economy, there is not much point sort of shifting powers and resources to the provinces because there is no stop. The pendulum will keep swinging until we end up with a community of communities or a federation of—a confederation of shopping centres, or whatever it is, and that is not my view of Canada. I thought we could build a strong Canada through co-operation. I have been disillusioned.

Trudeau's critics say that it is he who is directly responsible for the decline of cooperative federalism. Certainly he fought hard for the Charter and on other issues, as well, he bargained hard with the premiers. But, a Charter of Rights and Freedoms with a strengthened judiciary is not necessarily a bad thing, despite some premiers' apprehensions, and to attribute all that is perceived to be wrong with Canadian federalism to the negotiating style of one man is likely too simplistic an evaluation.

The seemingly irreconcilable differences between Ottawa and the provinces are the products of more weighty problems than one man's perceived personality flaws. Inflation, recession, the uncertain energy supply and price, and the interest rate policies of Canada's dominant trading partners have all heightened political anxiety and created a protectionist mentality at all levels of government. Quite simply, the economic pie has been steadily shrinking while government appetites have continued to grow. With less to go around the inevitable question is who will control what is available? Here the same two conflicting views of Canada that collided during the constitutional debate come head to head once again.

Tomorrow, however, they will meet in a changed arena, for those two views—federal and provincial, central and regional—have now been joined by a third view, that of the individual Canadian citizen. If federal-provincial relations were weakened during the long constitutional struggle, individual awareness of constitutional issues was strengthened. That same third voice, the Canadian people, that the judiciary must now recognize will also become a major participant in future constitutional negotiations. No longer will it be enough for Ottawa and the provinces to approach constitutional bargaining from the perspective of which level of government wants what area of jurisdiction, for no longer do interest groups sit passively by and allow such a process to occur. Now, a multitude of citizen groups will be pushing governments to approach constitutional reform from the point of view not of what is desirable for governments but of what is best for Canadians. The Charter of Rights and Freedoms with its protection for women, the handicapped, native peoples and all age groups is evidence that governments will set aside their differences when confronted by the demands of a united citizenry.

The Canada Act 1982

Whereas Canada has requested and consented to the enactment of an Act of the Parliament of the United Kingdom to give effect to the provisions hereinafter set forth and the Senate and the House of Commons of Canada in Parliament assembled have submitted an address to Her Majesty requesting that Her Majesty may graciously be pleased to cause a Bill to be laid before the Parliament of the United Kingdom for that purpose.

Be it therefore enacted by the Queen's Most Excellent Majesty, by and with the advice and consent of the Lords Spiritual and Temporal, and Commons, in this present Parliament assembled, and by the authority of the same, as follows:

1. The *Constitution Act, 1982* set out in Schedule B to this Act is hereby enacted for and shall have the force of law in Canada and shall come into force as provided in that Act.

2. No Act of the Parliament of the United Kingdom passed after the *Constitution Act, 1982* comes into force shall extend to Canada as part of its law.

3. So far as it is not contained in Schedule B, the French version of this Act is set out in Schedule A to this Act and has the same authority in Canada as the English version thereof.

4. This Act may be cited as the *Canada Act 1982*.

The Constitution Act 1982

PART 1   SCHEDULE B

CANADIAN CHARTER OF RIGHTS AND FREEDOMS

Whereas Canada is founded upon principles that recognize the supremacy of God and the rule of law:

Guarantee of Rights and Freedoms

1. The *Canadian Charter of Rights and Freedoms* guarantees the rights and freedoms set out in it subject only to such reasonable limits prescribed by law as can be demonstrably justified in a free and democratic society.

Fundamental Freedoms

2. Everyone has the following fundamental freedoms:

(a) freedom of conscience and religion;

(b) freedom of thought, belief, opinion and expression, including freedom of the press and other media of communication;

(c) freedom of peaceful assembly; and

(d) freedom of association.

Democratic Rights

3. Every citizen of Canada has the right to vote in an election of members of the House of Commons or of a legislative assembly and to be qualified for membership therein.

4. (1) No House of Commons and no legislative assembly shall continue for longer than five years from the date fixed for the return of the writs at a general election of its members.

(2) In time of real or apprehended war, invasion or insurrection, a House of Commons may be continued by Parliament and a legislative assembly may be continued by the legislature beyond five years if such continuation is not opposed by the votes of more than one-third of the members of the House of Commons or the legislative assembly, as the case may be.

5. There shall be a sitting of Parliament and of each legislature at least once every twelve months.

Mobility Rights

6. (1) Every citizen of Canada has the right to enter, remain in and leave Canada.

(2) Every citizen of Canada and every person who has the status of a permanent resident of Canada has the right

(a) to move to and take up residence in any province; and

(b) to pursue the gaining of a livelihood in any province.

(3) The rights specified in subsection (2) are subject to

(a) any laws or practices of general application in force in a province other than those that discriminate among persons primarily on the basis of province of present or previous residence; and

(b) any laws providing for reasonable residency requirements as a qualification for the receipt of publicly provided social services.

(4) Subsections (2) and (3) do not preclude any law, program or activity that has as its object the amelioration in a province of conditions of individuals in that province who are socially or economically disadvantaged if the rate of employment in that province is below the rate of employment in Canada.

Legal Rights

7. Everyone has the right to life, liberty and security of the person and the right not to be deprived thereof except in accordance with the principles of fundamental justice.

8. Everyone has the right to be secure against unreasonable search or seizure.

9. Everyone has the right not to be arbitrarily detained or imprisoned.

10. Everyone has the right on arrest or detention

(a) to be informed promptly of the reasons therefor;

(b) to retain and instruct counsel without delay and to be informed of that right; and

(c) to have the validity of the detention determined by way of *habeas corpus* and to be released if the detention is not lawful.

11. Any person charged with an offence has the right

(a) to be informed without unreasonable delay of the specific offence;

(b) to be tried within a reasonable time;

(c) not to be compelled to be a witness in proceedings against that person in respect of the offence;

(d) to be presumed innocent until proven guilty according to law in a fair and public hearing by an independent and impartial tribunal;

(e) not to be denied reasonable bail without just cause;

(f) except in the case of an offence under military law tried before a military

tribunal, to the benefit of trial by jury where the maximum punishment for the offence is imprisonment for five years or a more severe punishment;

(g) not to be found guilty on account of any act or omission unless, at the time of the act or omission, it constituted an offence under Canadian or international law or was criminal according to the general principles of law recognized by the community of nations;

(h) if finally acquitted of the offence, not to be tried for it again and, if finally found guilty and punished for the offence, not to be tried or punished for it again; and

(i) if found guilty of the offence and if the punishment for the offence has been varied between the time of commission and the time of sentencing, to the benefit of the lesser punishment.

12. Everyone has the right not to be subjected to any cruel and unusual treatment or punishment.

13. A witness who testifies in any proceedings has the right not to have any incriminating evidence so given used to incriminate that witness in any other proceedings, except in a prosecution for perjury or for the giving of contradictory evidence.

14. A party or witness in any proceedings who does not understand or speak the language in which the proceedings are conducted or who is deaf has the right to the assistance of an interpreter.

Equality Rights

15. (1) Every individual is equal before and under the law and has the right to the equal protection and equal benefit of the law without discrimination and, in particular, without discrimination based on race, national or ethnic origin, colour, religion, sex, age or mental or physical disability.

(2) Subsection (1) does not preclude any law, program or activity that has as its object the amelioration of conditions of disadvantaged individuals or groups including those that are disadvantaged because of race, national or ethnic origin, colour, religion, sex, age or mental or physical disability.

Official Languages of Canada

16. (1) English and French are the official languages of Canada and have equality of status and equal rights and privileges as to their use in all institutions of the Parliament and government of Canada.

(2) English and French are the official languages of New Brunswick and have equality of status and equal rights and privileges as to their use in all institutions of the legislature and government of New Brunswick.

(3) Nothing in this Charter limits the authority of Parliament or a legislature to advance the equality of status or use of English and French.

17. (1) Everyone has the right to use English or French in any debates and other proceedings of Parliament.

(2) Everyone has the right to use English or French in any debates and other proceedings of the legislature of New Brunswick.

18. (1) The statutes, records and journals of Parliament shall be printed and published in English and French and both language versions are equally authoritative.

(2) The statutes, records and journals of the legislature of New Brunswick shall be printed and published in English and French and both language versions are equally authoritative.

19. (1) Either English or French may be used by any person in, or in any pleading in or process issuing from, any court established by Parliament.

(2) Either English or French may be used by any person in, or in any pleading in or process issuing from, any court of New Brunswick.

20. (1) Any member of the public in Canada has the right to communicate with, and to receive available services from, any head or central office of an institution of the Parliament or government of Canada in English or French, and has the same right with respect to any other office of any such institution where

(a) there is a significant demand for communications with and services from that office in such language; or

(b) due to the nature of the office, it is reasonable that communications with and services from that office be available in both English and French.

(2) Any member of the public in New Brunswick has the right to communicate with, and to receive available services from, any office of an institution of the legislature or government of New Brunswick in English or French.

21. Nothing in sections 16 to 20 abrogates or derogates from any right, privilege or obligation with respect to the English and French languages, or either of them, that exists or is continued by virtue of any other provision of the Constitution of Canada.

22. Nothing in sections 16 to 20 abrogates or derogates from any legal or customary right or privilege acquired or enjoyed either before or after the coming into force of this Charter with respect to any language that is not English or French.

Minority Language Educational Rights

23. (1) Citizens of Canada

(a) whose first language learned and still understood is that of the English or French linguistic minority population of the province in which they reside, or

(b) who have received their primary school instruction in Canada in English or French and reside in a province where the language in which they received that instruction is the language of the English or French linguistic minority population of the province,

have the right to have their children receive primary and secondary school instruction in that language in that province.

(2) Citizens of Canada of whom any child has received or is receiving primary or secondary school instruction in English or French in Canada, have the right to have all their children receive primary and secondary school instruction in the same language.

(3) The right of citizens of Canada under subsections (1) and (2) to have their children receive primary and secondary school instruction in the language of the English or French linguistic minority population of a province

(a) applies wherever in the province the number of children of citizens who have such a right is sufficient to warrant the provision to them out of public funds of minority language instruction; and

(b) includes, where the number of those children so warrants, the right to have them receive that instruction in minority language educational facilities provided out of public funds.

Enforcement

24. (1) Anyone whose rights or freedoms, as guaranteed by this Charter, have been infringed or denied may apply to a court of competent jurisdiction to obtain such remedy as the court considers appropriate and just in the circumstances.

(2) Where, in proceedings under subsection (1), a court concludes that evidence was obtained in a manner that infringed or denied any rights or freedoms guaranteed by this Charter, the evidence shall be excluded if it is established that, having regard to all the circumstances, the admission of it in the proceedings would bring the administration of justice into disrepute.

General

25. The guarantee in this Charter of certain rights and freedoms shall not be construed so as to abrogate or derogate from any aboriginal, treaty or other rights or freedoms that pertain to the aboriginal peoples of Canada including

(a) any rights or freedoms that have been recognized by the Royal Proclamation of October 7, 1763; and

(b) any rights or freedoms that may be acquired by the aboriginal peoples of Canada by way of land claims settlement.

26. The guarantee in this Charter of certain rights and freedoms shall not be construed as denying the existence of any other rights or freedoms that exist in Canada.

27. This Charter shall be interpreted in a manner consistent with the preservation and enhancement of the multicultural heritage of Canadians.

28. Notwithstanding anything in this Charter, the rights and freedoms referred to in it are guaranteed equally to male and female persons.

29. Nothing in this Charter abrogates or derogates from any rights or privileges guaranteed by or under the Constitution of Canada in respect of denominational, separate or dissentient schools.

30. A reference in this Charter to a province or to the legislative assembly or legislature of a province shall be deemed to include a reference to the Yukon Territory and the Northwest Territories, or to the appropriate legislative authority thereof, as the case may be.

31. Nothing in this Charter extends the legislative powers of any body or authority.

Application of Charter

32. (1) This Charter applies

(a) to the Parliament and government of Canada in respect of all matters within the authority of Parliament including all matters relating to the Yukon Territory and Northwest Territories; and

(b) to the legislature and government of each province in respect of all matters within the authority of the legislature of each province.

(2) Notwithstanding subsection (1), section 15 shall not have effect until three years after this section comes into force.

33. (1) Parliament or the legislature of a province may expressly declare in an Act of Parliament or of the legislature, as the case may be, that the Act or a provision thereof shall operate notwithstanding a provision included in section 2 or sections 7 to 15 of this Charter.

(2) An Act or a provision of an Act in respect of which a declaration made under this section is in effect shall have such operation as it would have but for the provision of this Charter referred to in the declaration.

(3) A declaration made under subsection (1) shall cease to have effect five years after it comes into force or on such earlier date as may be specified in the declaration.

(4) Parliament or a legislature of a province may re-enact a declaration made under subsection (1).

(5) Subsection (3) applies in respect of a re-enactment made under subsection (4).

Citation

34. This Part may be cited as the *Canadian Charter of Rights and Freedoms*.

PART II

RIGHTS OF THE ABORIGINAL PEOPLES OF CANADA

35. (1) The existing aboriginal and treaty rights of the aboriginal peoples of Canada are hereby recognized and affirmed.

(2) In this Act, ''aboriginal peoples of Canada'' includes the Indian, Inuit and Métis peoples of Canada.

PART III

EQUALIZATION AND REGIONAL DISPARITIES

36. (1) Without altering the legislative authority of Parliament or of the provincial legislatures, or the rights of any of them with respect to the exercise of their legislative authority, Parliament and the legislatures, together with the government of Canada and the provincial governments, are committed to

(a) promoting equal opportunities for the well-being of Canadians;

(b) furthering economic development to reduce disparity in opportunities; and

(c) providing essential public services of reasonable quality to all Canadians.

(2) Parliament and the government of Canada are committed to the principle of making equalization payments to ensure that provincial governments have sufficient revenues to provide reasonably comparable levels of public services at reasonably comparable levels of taxation.

PART IV

CONSTITUTIONAL CONFERENCE

37. (1) A constitutional conference composed of the Prime Minister of Canada and the first ministers of the provinces shall be convened by the Prime Minister of Canada within one year after this Part comes into force.

(2) The conference convened under subsection (1) shall have included in its agenda an item respecting constitutional matters that directly affect the aboriginal peoples of Canada, including the identification and definition of the rights of those peoples to be included in the Constitution of Canada, and the Prime Minister of Canada shall invite representatives of those peoples to participate in the discussions on that item.

(3) The Prime Minister of Canada shall invite elected representatives of the governments of the Yukon Territory and the Northwest Territories to participate in the discussions on any item on the agenda of the conference convened under subsection (1) that, in the opinion of the Prime Minister, directly affects the Yukon Territory and the Northwest Territories.

PART V

PROCEDURE FOR AMENDING CONSTITUTION OF CANADA

38. (1) An amendment to the Constitution of Canada may be made by proclamation issued by the Governor General under the Great Seal of Canada where so authorized by

(a) resolutions of the Senate and House of Commons; and

(b) resolutions of the legislative assemblies of at least two-thirds of the provinces that have, in the aggregate, according to the then latest general census, at least fifty per cent of the population of all the provinces.

(2) An amendment made under subsection (1) that derogates from the legislative powers, the proprietary rights or any other rights or privileges of the legislature or government of a province shall require a resolution supported by a majority of the members of each of the Senate, the House of Commons and the legislative assemblies required under subsection (1).

(3) An amendment referred to in subsection (2) shall not have effect in a province the legislative assembly of which has expressed its dissent thereto by resolution supported by a majority of its members prior to the issue of the proclamation to which the amendment relates unless that legislative assembly, subsequently, by resolution supported by a majority of its members, revokes its dissent and authorizes the amendment.

(4) A resolution of dissent made for the purposes of subsection (3) may be revoked at any time before or after the issue of the proclamation to which it relates.

39. (1) A proclamation shall not be issued under subsection 38(1) before the expiration of one year from the adoption of the resolution initiating the amendment procedure thereunder, unless the legislative assembly of each province has previously adopted a resolution of assent or dissent.

(2) A proclamation shall not be issued under subsection 38(1) after the expiration of three years from the adoption of the resolution initiating the amendment procedure thereunder.

40. Where an amendment is made under subsection 38(1) that transfers provincial legislative powers relating to education or other cultural matters from provincial legislatures to Parliament, Canada shall provide reasonable compensation to any province to which the amendment does not apply.

41. An amendment to the Constitution of Canada in relation to the following matters may be made by proclamation issued by the Governor General under the Great Seal of Canada only where authorized by resolutions of the Senate and House of Commons and of the legislative assembly of each province:

(a) the office of the Queen, the Governor General and the Lieutenant Governor of a province;

(b) the right of a province to a number of members in the House of Commons not less than the number of Senators by which the province is entitled to be represented at the time this Part comes into force;

(c) subject to section 43, the use of the English or the French language;

(d) the composition of the Supreme Court of Canada; and

(e) an amendment to this Part.

42. (1) An amendment to the Constitution of Canada in relation to the following matters may be made only in accordance with subsection 38(1):

(a) the principle of proportionate representation of the provinces in the House of Commons prescribed by the Constitution of Canada;

(b) the powers of the Senate and the method of selecting Senators;

(c) the number of members by which a province is entitled to be represented in the Senate and the residence qualifications of Senators;

(d) subject to paragraph 41(d), the Supreme Court of Canada;

(e) the extension of existing provinces into the territories; and

(f) notwithstanding any other law or practice, the establishment of new provinces.

(2) Subsections 38(2) to (4) do not apply in respect of amendments in relation to matters referred to in subsection (1).

43. An amendment to the Constitution of Canada in relation to any provision that applies to one or more, but not all, provinces, including

(a) any alteration to boundaries between provinces, and

(b) any amendment to any provision that relates to the use of the English or the French language within a province,

may be made by proclamation issued by the Governor General under the Great Seal of Canada only where so authorized by resolutions of the Senate and House of Commons and of the legislative assembly of each province to which the amendment applies.

44. Subject to section 41 and 42, Parliament may exclusively make laws amending the Constitution of Canada in relation to the executive government of Canada or the Senate and House of Commons.

45. Subject to section 41, the legislature of each province may exclusively make laws amending the constitution of the province.

46. (1) The procedures for amendment under sections 38, 41, 42 and 43 may be initiated either by the Senate or the House of Commons or by the legislative assembly of a province.

(2) A resolution of assent made for the purposes of this Part may be revoked at any time before the issue of a proclamation authorized by it.

47. (1) An amendment to the Constitution of Canada made by proclamation under section 38, 41, 42 or 43 may be made without a resolution of the Senate authorizing the issue of the proclamation if, within one hundred and eighty days after the adoption by the House of Commons of a resolution authorizing its issue, the Senate has not adopted such a resolution and if, at any time after the expiration of that period, the House of Commons again adopts the resolution.

(2) Any period when Parliament is prorogued or dissolved shall not be counted in computing the one hundred and eighty day period referred to in subsection (1).

48. The Queen's Privy Council for Canada shall advise the Governor General to issue a proclamation under this Part forthwith on the adoption of the resolutions required for an amendment made by proclamation under this Part.

49. A constitutional conference composed of the Prime Minister of Canada and the first ministers of the provinces shall be convened by the Prime Minister of Canada within fifteen years after this Part comes into force to review the provisions of this Part.

PART VI

AMENDMENT TO THE CONSTITUTION ACT, 1867

50. The *Constitution Act, 1867* (formerly named the *British North America Act, 1867*) is amended by adding thereto, immediately after section 92 thereof, the following heading and section:

"Non-Renewable Natural Resources, Forestry Resources and Electrical Energy

92A. (1) In each province, the legislature may exclusively make laws in relation to

(a) exploration for non-renewable natural resources in the province;

(b) development, conservation and management of non-renewable natural resources and forestry resources in the province, including laws in relation to the rate of primary production therefrom; and

(c) development, conservation and management of sites and facilities in the province for the generation and production of electrical energy.

(2) In each province, the legislature may make laws in relation to the export from the province to another part of Canada of the primary production from non-renewable natural resources and forestry resources in the province and the production from facilities in the province for the generation of electrical energy, but such laws may not authorize or provide for discrimination in prices or in supplies exported to another part of Canada.

(3) Nothing in subsection (2) derogates from the authority of Parliament to

enact laws in relation to the matters referred to in that subsection and, where such a law of Parliament and a law of a province conflict, the law of Parliament prevails to the extent of the conflict.

(4) In each province, the legislature may make laws in relation to the raising of money by any mode or system of taxation in respect of

(a) non-renewable natural resources and forestry resources in the province and the primary production therefrom, and

(b) sites and facilities in the province for the generation of electrical energy and the production therefrom,

whether or not such production is exported in whole or in part from the province, but such laws may not authorize or provide for taxation that differentiates between production exported to another part of Canada and production not exported from the province.

(5) The expression "primary production" has the meaning assigned by the Sixth Schedule.

(6) Nothing in subsections (1) to (5) derogates from any powers or rights that a legislature or government of a province had immediately before the coming into force of this section."

51. The said Act is further amended by adding thereto the following Schedule:

"THE SIXTH SCHEDULE

Primary Production from Non-Renewable Natural Resources and Forestry Resources

1. For the purposes of section 92A of this Act,

(a) production from a non-renewable natural resource is primary production therefrom if

(i) it is in the form in which it exists upon its recovery or severance from its natural state, or

(ii) it is a product resulting from processing or refining the resource, and is not a manufactured product or a product resulting from refining crude oil, refining upgraded heavy crude oil, refining gases or liquids derived from coal or refining a synthetic equivalent of crude oil; and

(b) production from a forestry resource is primary production therefrom if it consists of sawlogs, poles, lumber, wood chips, sawdust or any other primary wood product, or wood pulp, and is not a product manufactured from wood."

PART VII

GENERAL

52. (1) The Constitution of Canada is the supreme law of Canada, and any law that is inconsistent with the provisions of the Constitution is, to the extent of the inconsistency, of no force or effect.

(2) The Constitution of Canada includes

(a) the *Canada Act 1982*, including this Act;

(b) the Acts and orders referred to in Schedule I; and

(c) any amendment to any Act or order referred to in paragraph *(a)* or *(b)*.

(3) Amendments to the Constitution of Canada shall be made only in accordance with the authority contained in the Constitution of Canada.

53. (1) The enactments referred to in Column I of Schedule I are hereby repealed or amended to the extent indicated in Column II thereof and, unless repealed, shall continue as law in Canada under the names set out in Column III thereof.

(2) Every enactment, except the *Canada Act 1982*, that refers to an enactment referred to in Schedule I by the name in Column I thereof is hereby amended by substituting for that name the corresponding name in Column III thereof, and any British North America Act not referred to in Schedule I may be cited as the *Constitution Act* followed by the year and number, if any, of its enactment.

54. Part IV is repealed on the day that is one year after this Part comes into force and this section may be repealed and this Act renumbered, consequential upon the repeal of Part IV and this section, by proclamation issued by the Governor General under the Great Seal of Canada.

55. A French version of the portions of the Constitution of Canada referred to in Schedule I shall be prepared by the Minister of Justice of Canada as expeditiously as possible and, when any portion thereof sufficient to warrant action being taken has been so prepared, it shall be put forward for enactment by proclamation issued by the Governor General under the Great Seal of Canada pursuant to the procedure then applicable to an amendment of the same provisions of the Constitution of Canada.

56. Where any portion of the Constitution of Canada has been or is enacted in English and French or where a French version of any portion of the Constitution is enacted pursuant to section 55, the English and French versions of that portion of the Constitution are equally authoritative.

57. The English and French versions of this Act are equally authoritative.

58. Subject to section 59, this Act shall come into force on a day to be fixed by proclamation issued by the Queen or the Governor General under the Great Seal of Canada.

59. (1) Paragraph 23(1)*(a)* shall come into force in respect of Quebec on a day to be fixed by proclamation issued by the Queen or the Governor General under the Great Seal of Canada.

(2) A proclamation under subsection (1) shall be issued only where authorized by the legislative assembly or government of Quebec.

(3) This section may be repealed on the day paragraph 23(1)*(a)* comes into force in respect of Quebec and this Act amended and renumbered, consequential upon the repeal of this section, by proclamation issued by the Queen or the Governor General under the Great Seal of Canada.

60. This Act may be cited as the *Constitution Act, 1982*, and the Constitution Acts 1867 to 1975 (No. 2) and this Act may be cited together as the *Constitution Acts, 1867 to 1982*.

Index